NIGEL DAVIES

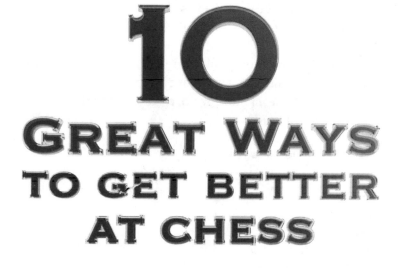

10
GREAT WAYS
TO GET BETTER
AT CHESS

EVERYMAN CHESS
www.everymanchess.com

First published in 2010 by Gloucester Publishers plc (formerly Everyman Publishers plc), Northburgh House, 10 Northburgh Street, London EC1V 0AT

IE 8.18 ? over my head

British Library Cataloguing-in-Publication Data
A catalogue record for this book is available from the British Library.

ISBN: 978 1 85744 633 3

Distributed in North America by The Globe Pequot Press, P.O Box 480, 246 Goose Lane, Guilford, CT 06437-0480.

All other sales enquiries should be directed to Everyman Chess, Northburgh House, 10 Northburgh Street, London EC1V 0AT
tel: 020 7253 7887 fax: 020 7490 3708
email: info@everymanchess.com; website: www.everymanchess.com

Everyman is the registered trade mark of Random House Inc. and is used in this work under licence from Random House Inc.

Dedicated to the determined improver.

Everyman Chess Series
Chief advisor: Byron Jacobs
Commissioning editor: John Emms
Assistant editor: Richard Palliser

Typeset and edited by First Rank Publishing, Brighton.
Cover design by Horatio Monteverde.
Printed and bound in the US by Versa Press.

Contents

Bibliography

Books

Lasker's Greatest Chess Games 1889-1914, Fred Reinfeld & Reuben Fine (Dover 1963)

Lasker's Manual of Chess, Emanuel Lasker (Printing-Craft Limited 1932)

Nimzowitsch: A Reappraisal, Raymond Keene (Batsford 1999; first published 1974)

One Hundred Selected Games, Mikhail Botvinnik (Dover 2003; first published 1960)

Pawn Power in Chess, Hans Kmoch (Dover 1991; first published 1959)

Sahovski Olympiad Havana 1966 (Sahovski Informator 1966)

The Art of the Middle Game, Paul Keres & Alexander Kotov (Penguin 1964)

The Guardian Chess Book, Leonard Barden (Hodder & Stoughton Ltd 1967)

The Middle Years of Paul Keres, Paul Keres (Herbert Jenkins 1966)

The Right Way to Play Chess, Imre König (Barnes & Noble Books 1979)

Think Like a Grandmaster, Alexander Kotov (Batsford 1971)

World Chess Championship: Korchnoi vs. Karpov: The Inside Story of the Match, Raymond Keene (Simon & Schuster 1978)

Zoom 001: Zero Hour to the Operation of Opening Models, Steffen Zeuthen and Bent Larsen (Dansk Skakforlag 1979)

Software and Databases

ChessBase 10

Fritz 12

Megabase 2010

Introduction

The ways people approach the task of trying to improve their chess can be haphazard at the best of times. This is particularly the case at amateur level, where players tend to have far less time and energy available. The demands of having a job and family mean that it's hard to get better even if the time available for chess is directed with filigree precision. And players in this position can ill afford the numerous false starts that full-time chess addicts are able to devote to the process.

So there is a genuine need for direction on the matter of chess improvement, yet answers are difficult to find in existing literature. There have been a huge number of books written about the game, yet the authors tend to stop short of explaining that if a club level player does X, Y and Z he will improve.

Perhaps this dearth of direct answers has led to the belief that it is impossible for someone to improve their chess after a certain age. Frankly, I believe this view is total poppycock; players can improve their chess at any age as long as they adopt an effective approach.

So my remit in this volume is clear; I will be showing you ten great ways to improve your chess while being as explicit as possible about what you should do. To this end I have drawn heavily on the games and thoughts of players who have been my students over the years and experienced a clear improvement in their game.

Not all of these methods will work equally well for every player, and in my work with students there is usually a focus on one or two which I think will be of most benefit. They also need to be acted upon, which is where many people fall down. It is one thing to know how to do something in theory and quite another to put it into practice.

The determined individuals I have worked with deserve all the credit for succeeding in this process, especially amidst the constraints of job and family commitments. But I like to think that I might have helped light the way, and my hope is that these improvement methods may help a wider audience.

Nigel Davies,
Southport,
June 2010

Chapter One

Develop Your Vision

"Played as it was in the first round, this game showed me that I possessed at Liége the primary condition for success in a tournament, which is the power to see clear and deep." – Saviely Tartakower (*My Best Games of Chess: 1905-1930*)

The most important attribute for any chess player is the ability to calculate variations quickly and accurately. Without this it becomes very difficult to discuss the finer points of strategy, such as pawn structure and planning, because what good is a better structure if one is down a piece? And most games, even at Grandmaster level, are decided when one of the players sees something that the other one misses.

Anyone who doubts the truth of this should look at the following example in which even a former World Champion, Anatoly Karpov, misses a simple fork of two of his pieces. So how many more oversights like this lie a few moves behind the scenes?

Game 1
L.Christiansen-A.Karpov
Wijk aan Zee 1993
Queen's Indian Defence

1 d4 ♘f6 2 c4 e6 3 ♘f3 b6 4 a3

Many exponents of this line prefer the move order 4 ♘c3 ♗b7 5 a3 in order to avoid various 4th move alternatives such as 4...♗a6. This allows Black an alternative of his own in 4...♗b4, which leads to quite double-edged play.

4...♗a6 5 ♕c2 ♗b7 6 ♘c3 c5 7 e4 cxd4

Reaching a kind of Sicilian position, and one which is fine for Black.

8 ♘xd4 ♘c6 9 ♘xc6 ♗xc6 10 ♗f4 ♘h5 11 ♗e3 ♗d6??

This move has sophisticated undertones, such as control of dark squares like e5 and f4. Yet Black has overlooked that the bishop on d6 and knight on h5 are vulnerable to a simple fork:

12 ♕d1! 1-0

I wonder if this move escaped Karpov's awareness because it was a retreat? These are notoriously difficult to spot, especially backwards knight moves.

You might think, of course, that this was just a freak accident, so let me show you another game by another World Champion, this time Garry Kasparov in a game against Judit Polgar:

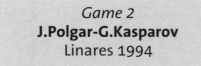

Game 2
J.Polgar-G.Kasparov
Linares 1994

The position in the diagram arose after White's 36th move. This incident has been likened to Maradona's 'Hand of God' football episode.

Kasparov played 36...♘c5, according to some reports let the piece go, and then played it to f8 instead. The problem is that 36...♘c5 cuts off the rook's guard of the c6-square and allows the immediately decisive 37 ♗c6. Instead the game continued as follows, with Kasparov eventually going on to win:

36...♘f8?

36...♖b8! was much stronger.

37 ♘e4 ♘8d7 38 ♘xf6+ ♘xf6 39 ♕xb6 ♘g4! 40 ♖f1

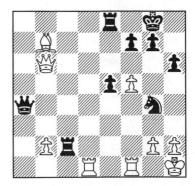

40...e4?

Missing 40...♘f2+!, after which 41 ♖xf2 ♖xf2 threatens White's rook on d1 with the queen.

41 ♗d5 e3! 42 ♗b3 ♛e4!

Threatening mate on g2, so White has to take the rook.

43 ♗xc2 ♛xc2 44 ♖d8 ♖xd8 45 ♛xd8+ ♚h7 46 ♛e7 ♛c4! 0-1

When the rook moves away from the f-file Black has 47...♛f4.

Look through other games, especially with *Fritz* or *Rybka*, and similar mistakes will be found. I rest my case that nobody is immune to this kind of error and it plays a huge part in the outcomes.

Unfortunately it also seems that vision is the aspect of chess which is most dependent on innate talent. I've found that it's quite difficult for those who are not naturally gifted in this department to progress beyond a certain level, though there are things that can be done to develop vision.

In my teenage years I spent many hours looking at complex positions from autobiographical games collections such as those of Paul Keres. I would give myself a certain amount of time on the clock, write down everything that I saw and then compare it with what was analysed in the book. There are very few people who are prepared to do this kind of work, but there's no doubt in my mind that it helped my game considerably.

A slightly toned down version of this kind of exercise is to spend some time solving positions from chess puzzle books or computer programs. The best way is to solve the positions directly from the diagram itself rather than waste time setting up the positions on a board.

Blindfold chess is another good way to try and develop vision. Most club level players will have difficulty conducting an entire game without looking at the board, but there is a mini-blindfold exercise that should prove beneficial: while playing through a game on a board you can write down the position as you 'see' it a certain number of moves hence.

Case History: Derrick Jones

In 2003 Derrick Jones (then aged 37) was rated below 1000, but over the next few years moved up by some 400 points largely through an improvement in his tactical vision. Here are four examples of his play, the first two from 2003, the next two from 2009. There is a huge difference in the extent of his chessboard vision, which accounts for every point of the Elo rating increase.

Game 3
D.W.Jones-P.Curr
Leek Congress 2005

We join the first game after 23 moves in what looks like a fairly level position. In fact the fun is just beginning as we get to the business end of the action.

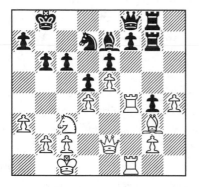

24 ♘a4? ♔b7?

Black should play 24...♗xa3, when 25 bxa3 ♕xa3+ gets the bishop on g3.
25 ♖h1 ♖g6 26 ♔b1 ♕g7 27 ♖hf1 ♖f8 28 ♖1f2 ♕g8 29 ♕f1 ♖g7 30 h5?

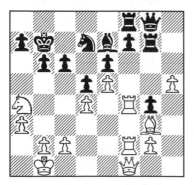

Allowing Black's powerful reply.

30...♗g5 31 ♖xg4

31...♗h6??

This time missing 31...♗e3, when 32 ♖xg7 ♕xg7 33 ♖f3 ♗xd4 would be very good for Black.
32 ♖xg7 ♕xg7 33 ♗h4 ♗g5? 34 ♗xg5 ♕xg5

35 ♕h1?

Another missed opportunity. 35 ♖xf7 wins a crucial pawn for nothing and leaves White with a killer passed h-pawn.
35...♕h6?

35...♕g4 is the move, hitting d4.
36 ♕h4 f5? 37 ♖f4

37 ♕e7! is strong.

37...♖g8 38 ♖f2 ♕e3?

38...♖g5! is stronger, keeping White's queen out and hitting the pawn on h5.

39 h6 ♖g4 40 ♕e7 ♕xf2 41 ♕xd7+ ♔a6?

41...♔b8 is a better try; the text should lose by force.

42 h7?

White can win with the spectacular 42 ♘c5+ ♔b5 (42...bxc5 43 ♕xc6+ ♔a5 44 ♕xc5+ ♔a6 45 ♕c6+ ♔a5 46 b4 mate) 43 a4+ ♔c4 44 ♘b3 ♕g1+ 45 ♔a2 ♕xd4 46 ♕xc6+ ♕c5 47 ♘xc5 etc.

42...♖h4??

42...♕f1+ 43 ♔a2 ♕c4+ 44 ♔b1 ♕f1+ draws by repetition.

43 ♕c8+ ♔b5 44 ♘c3+ ♔c4 45 ♕xc6+??

45 h8♕ is just winning.

45...♔xd4 46 ♘b5+ ♔xe5??

46...♔e4 is correct.

47 ♕c3+?

47 ♕d6+ ♔f6 48 ♕d8+ ♔g6 49 ♕g8+ ♔f6 50 h8♕+ is winning.

47...d4 48 ♕c7+ ♔e4 49 ♘d6+ ♔e3[3] 50 ♕g7 ♖h1+ 51 ♔a2 ♕h4 52 ♕xa7 ♕xh7 53 ♕xb6 ♕h5?

53...♕d7 is better.

54 ♕b3+ ♔f4 55 a4?

55 ♕xe6 leaves Black in all sorts of trouble.

55...♕d1 56 g3+ ♔g4

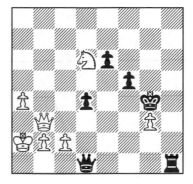

57 ♔a3?

57 ♕xe6 would have made a fight of it.

57...♕f3 58 ♘c4?!

Losing quickly. 58 ♕xf3+ ♔xf3 59 b4 would have put up more resistance.

58...♕xb3+ 59 ♔xb3 ♔xg3 60 a5 f4 61 a6 f3 62 a7 ♖h8 0-1

Game 4
F.Frost-D.W.Jones
Leek Congress 2005
Réti Opening

1 ♘f3 ♘f6 2 g3 d5 3 ♗g2 c6 4 d3 ♗g4 5 0-0 ♘bd7 6 ♘bd2 e5 7 ♖e1

Excessive preparation. If White wants to put his pawn on e4 he should do it immediately with 7 e4.

Another plan is 7 c4; for example, 7...♗d6 8 h3 ♗h5 9 cxd5 cxd5 10 e4 0-0

11 exd5 ♘xd5 12 ♕b3 ♘5f6 13 ♘e4
♘xe4 14 dxe4 ♘c5 15 ♕d5 ♗xf3 16
♗xf3 ♕f6 17 ♗g2 ♖fd8 18 ♗e3 was
about equal in D.Norwood-M.Adams,
British Championship, Plymouth 1989.

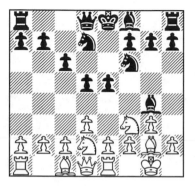

7...♗d6

Black can exploit the dark side of
White's last move with 7...e4; for example, 8 dxe4 dxe4 9 ♘g5 e3 10 fxe3
♕e7 11 ♘b3 0-0-0 gives Black strong
pressure for the pawn.

8 e4 0-0 9 ♘f1 h6 10 c3 ♗c5 11 h3 ♗e6

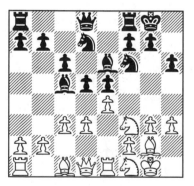

I guess Black hadn't seen the indi-
rect defences for his e-pawn at this
stage, in which case he should probably
take on e4 first.

12 b4

It turns out that 12 exd5 ♘xd5 13
♘xe5 is met by 13...♗xf2+ 14 ♔xf2
♘xe5 15 ♖xe5 ♕f6+ winning the rook.
**12...♗b6 13 exd5 cxd5 14 ♘xe5 ♘xe5
15 ♖xe5**

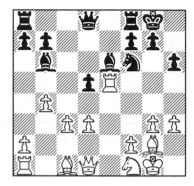

15...♖c8?!

Black should fork the pawns on c3
and h3 with 15...♕c8 16 ♗b2 ♗xh3.

**16 ♗d2 ♗c7 17 ♖e2 ♖e8 18 ♗e3 ♕d7
19 ♔h2 ♘g4+??**

Whoops, this is a whole piece!
19...♗e5 is the correct move.

**20 hxg4 ♗xg4 21 f3 ♗e6 22 ♕d2 ♗d8
23 g4 ♗f6 24 ♖c1 ♕e7 25 ♘g3 ♗e5 26
♗xa7??**

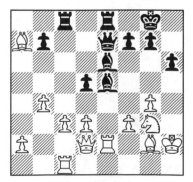

OK, well, White hasn't played it very convincingly over the last few moves but here he blunders. 26 ♗f4 still wins. **26...♕h4+ 27 ♔g1 ♗xg3 28 ♗f2 ♗xf2+ 29 ♖xf2 ♖c6 30 ♖e1 ♖ec8 31 ♖c1 h5 32 ♗h1?**

Giving away his g-pawn. 32 g5 is better.

32...hxg4 33 ♖h2?

Mistakes often come in groups. 33 fxg4 is relatively best.

33...♕g3+ 34 ♖g2 ♕e5 35 d4 ♕f5

35...♕c7 gets the c3-pawn.

36 ♖xg4 ♕h5 37 ♖g3 ♗f5 38 f4 ♖h6?

38...♖g6 was the right move; for example, 39 ♖xg6 ♕xg6+ 40 ♕g2 ♕e6 gives Black the better chances because of White's exposed king.

39 ♕g2??

White can take Black's d-pawn while defending himself with 39 ♗xd5. From here on he doesn't get another chance.

39...♗e4 40 ♖xg7+ ♔h8 41 ♕g3 ♕xh1+ 42 ♔f2 ♕xc1 43 ♖xf7 ♗g6 44 ♖f6 ♕c2+ 45 ♔f3 ♖xc3+ 46 ♔g4 ♖xg3+ 47 ♔xg3 ♕d3+ 48 ♔g4 ♕h3+ 49 ♔g5 ♕h4 mate

Clearly there were a lot of tactical oversights and mistakes here, but make no mistake that this is what happens around 1000 Elo. Reduce their prevalence and the result is simply magic: players' grades go up hugely! And without learning a single chess opening.

Game 5
D.W.Jones-S.Nixon
North Staffs League 2009
Queen's Pawn Opening

1 d4 d5 2 ♘f3 ♘c6 3 ♗f4

I really want to point out that we're already well clear of the main lines of theory, with the opening being a London System vs. the Chigorin Defence. This is typical of club chess and shows the lack of value in memorizing openings; sensible development is the order of the day.

3...♘f6 4 h3 ♘e4?! 5 ♘bd2 e6 6 e3 ♗d6 7 ♗xd6 ♕xd6

8 c3

I would mess Black's pawns up with 8 ♘xe4 dxe4 9 ♘d2, before he exchanged on d2 or played 8...f5.

8...h6?!

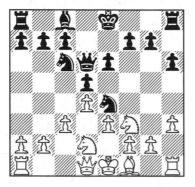

9 ♗d3

9 ♘xe4! dxe4 10 ♘d2 is even better than on the previous move, because 10...f5 can be answered by 11 ♕h5+ and Black can't play 11...g6 (his 8...h6 stopped that).

9...f5 10 ♗b5 ♗d7 11 ♗xc6 ♗xc6 12 0-0 0-0-0 13 ♘e5

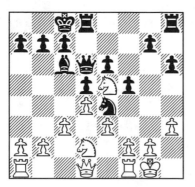

A nice knight against a not so nice bishop. But this won't be what wins White the game...

13...♗e8 14 ♘xe4 dxe4 15 ♕e2 g5 16 f3

♖h7?

16...exf3 is playable, not least because his bishop is starting to look a lot better. This, by the way, is why White should probably have played 16 c4.

17 fxe4 g4?

17...fxe4 18 ♕g4 wins a pawn, but not more than that.

18 hxg4 fxg4 19 ♕xg4 ♕b6 20 ♖f2 h5 21 ♕g8 ♖h6 22 ♖f8 ♕xb2

23 ♖xe8!

This move shows a really terrific improvement in Derrick's tactical ability. He's happy to let the rook go because he's winning the one on d8.

23...♕xa1+ 24 ♔h2 b6 25 ♖xd8+ ♔b7 26 ♖a8 ♕xc3 27 ♕c8 mate

This next game reminds me of a boxing movie I once saw in which a street fighter, having had years of training, is given a fight against someone of his earlier standard. After he wins easily his trainer pointed out that he'd essentially beaten someone not dissimilar to his old self, thus emphasizing the value of training.

Game 6
E.Scattergood-D.W.Jones
North Staffs League 2010
Caro-Kann Defence

1 e4 c6 2 ♘f3 d5 3 exd5

This is a typical reaction to the Caro-Kann from players who are meeting it for the first time.

3...cxd5 4 ♘c3

The knight is not well placed here because it is a full four moves from White's natural outpost on the half-open e-file (the e5-square). Of course this kind of slight error is entirely in keeping with the knights before bishops policy that many books offer.

4...♘f6 5 d4 a6

This kind of unnecessary prophylactic move (directed against possible checks on b5) is typical of players who lack tactical confidence, so tactics have an impact on players' strategic understanding. Black could and should just develop the other knight.

6 ♗d3 ♗g4 7 h3 ♗xf3 8 ♕xf3 ♘c6 9 0-0?

Blundering away the d4-pawn.

9...♘xd4 10 ♕e3 ♘c6 11 ♖d1? d4

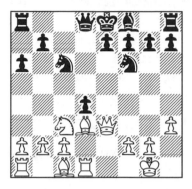

Winning a piece, essentially for nothing.

12 ♕f3 dxc3 13 bxc3 ♕c7 14 ♗f4 e5 15 ♖e1 ♗d6 16 ♗g3 0-0 17 ♗h4 ♗e7 18 ♕g3 ♖fe8 19 ♗g5 ♕d6 20 f4 ♘d7 21 ♗h6??

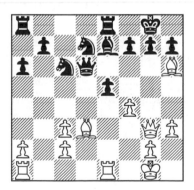

21...♕xh6

White is rapidly running out of pieces...

22 fxe5 ♘cxe5

22....♗h4 might have gotten her to throw in the towel.

23 ♖xe5 ♘xe5 24 ♕xe5 ♗f6 25 ♕d5 ♖ad8 26 ♕b3 ♕e3+ 27 ♔h1 ♕e7

27...♗e5, intending 28...♕g3, would probably have been quicker.
28 ♖f1 ♗h4 29 ♗c4 ♖f8 30 ♕a4? b5 31 ♕b3 bxc4 32 ♕xc4 ♖d2 33 ♕f4 ♕e2 34 ♖g1 ♗f2 35 ♖b1 ♖d1+ 36 ♖xd1 ♕xd1+ 37 ♔h2 ♕g1 mate

This was an efficient game on Black's part and underlines the progress he has made.

I think that Derrick's example shows the value of players applying themselves to the process of improvement, in his case the result being a 400-point improvement from his late 30s onwards, and I think that further progress is well within his capabilities. An improvement in a player's vision is likely to produce this kind of effect simply because it is so central to the chess-playing process.

What if a player has consistently tried to improve their chessboard vision but finds that he has reached a point of diminishing returns with this approach? Then I suggest, instead, that you use the other blunderbuss in the improvement arsenal, which is to study the endgame. While I don't think the effect is quite as dramatic, there are still huge gains to be made by studying the endgame. Remarkably, these are quite unrelated to actually reaching endgames in your games, and endgame skill is something that does not

require as much talent to acquire.

Key Points

1. Visualization skills are the most important aspect of chess strength, so they should be developed as far as possible via tactical and blindfold exercises. This should be the first port of call for anyone who wishes to improve their chess.

2. As this work progresses make a tally of whether your games are being won or lost in tactical situations. This calls for a large serving of self-honesty, even if you are doing the count quite scientifically.

3. If it is quite clear that you are winning most of the tactical slugfests that occur in your games, you may wish to make tactical play the central aspect of your game. Consider playing openings which lead to sharp positions.

4. If, on the other hand, no further progress is being made after 6-12 months of tactical training, it is likely that you are at a point of diminishing or zero returns. If you are still losing games through tactical mistakes, try to dampen the tactical potential of your games via astute opening choices (for example, Queen's Pawn Openings as White, and the French Defence and Queen's Gambit Declined as Black are suitable choices) and focus on developing endgame skill.

Chapter Two

Study the Endgame

Studying the endgame has been recommended by the likes of Anatoly Karpov and Jose Capablanca, so most of us have heard that we should do so. Yet very few people follow this advice, the excuses varying from a denial that they ever get into endgames to an admission that they find them boring. Unfortunately for them they are missing out on one of the most effective improvement methods; endgame study is useful on many different levels.

The first and most obvious function is to play them better, and this tends to be highly effective at club level. The endgame is the weakest side of most club level players, so a knowledge of this part of the game can be a devastating weapon. One strong club player that I knew liked to say that, if all else failed, he would exchange queens, which invariably increased his chances of winning.

Here are a couple examples of club level endgames, which show how they can be such a happy hunting ground. In both cases a lack of knowledge of the basics turns a winning position into a losing one.

Game 7
J.Thomas-N.Martin
London 1997

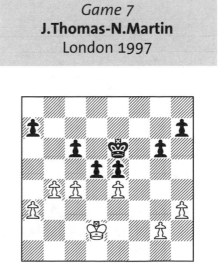

In this first example Jeff Thomas,

playing White, has found himself in what could have been an unpleasant situation. In the event he actually wins the game because he understood pawn endgames far better than his opponent.

1...dxe4??

Turning a winning position into a lost one with a single move. Had Black devoted some time to studying the endgame he would surely have played 1...d4, setting up a protected passed pawn. Play might continue 2 a4 (and not 2 b5? cxb5 3 cxb5 ♔d6 4 ♔d3 ♔c5 5 a4 ♔b4, when Black rounds up White's queenside pawns without further ado) 2...♔d7 (the immediate 2...c5 3 b5 ♔d7 allows White to keep Black's king out with 4 a5) 3 h4 ♔c7 4 g4 ♔b7

5 c5 (neither can White save himself with 5 a5 ♔a6 6 ♔c2 c5 7 ♔b3 cxb4 8 ♔xb4 d3 9 ♔c3 ♔xa5 10 ♔xd3 ♔b4, or 5 g5 c5 6 b5 ♔b6 followed by 7...♔a5) 5...a5 6 b5 cxb5 7 axb5 a4 8 ♔c2 a3 9 ♔b3 d3 and Black wins.

2 ♔e3 a6

Or if 2...♔f5 then 3 a4 a6 4 b5, when

the passed pawn White gets on the queenside will draw the black king away, much as in the game.

3 ♔xe4 ♔d6 4 a4!

Getting ready to create the winning passed pawn.

4...h6 5 b5 cxb5 6 cxb5 a5

Eliminating the queenside pawns wouldn't help Black either. After the continuation 6...axb5 7 axb5 ♔c5 8 ♔xe5 ♔xb5 9 ♔f6 White mops up the kingside.

7 h4!

A very classy move which makes the win relatively straightforward. White can also play 7 b6, but after 7...♔c6 8 ♔xe5 ♔xb6 he would need to find 9 ♔d6! (9 ♔f6 ♔c5 10 ♔xg6 ♔b4 11 ♔xh6 ♔xa4 12 g4 ♔b4 13 g5 a4 14 g6 a3 15 g7 a2 16 g8♕ a1♕ gives rise to a difficult, and theoretically drawn, queen endgame) 9...♔b7 10 ♔c5 ♔a6 11 ♔c6 ♔a7 12 ♔b5, when White will take the a-pawn and march over to the kingside to mop up the pawns over there.

7...♔e6 8 g4 ♔d6 9 h5 g5

9...gxh5 is no better; for example, 10 gxh5 ♔e6 11 b6 ♔d6 12 b7 ♔c7 13 ♔xe5 ♔xb7 14 ♔f6 ♔c7 (or 14...♔b6 15 ♔g6 ♔c5 16 ♔xh6 ♔b4 17 ♔g6 ♔xa4 18 h6 ♔b3 19 h7 a4 20 h8♕ a3 21 ♕a1, when the approach of White's king will win the a-pawn and the game) 15 ♔g6 ♔d7 16 ♔xh6 ♔e7 17 ♔g7 and the h-pawn queens.

10 b6!

Finally Black's king is drawn away and this time the win is easy.

10...♔c6 11 b7

11 ♔xe5 ♔xb6 12 ♔d6 would also win because Black would lose his a5-pawn after 12...♔a6 13 ♔c6 ♔a7 14 ♔b5 etc.

11...♔xb7 12 ♔xe5 ♔c6 13 ♔f6 ♔c5 14 ♔g6 ♔b4 15 ♔xh6 ♔xa4 16 ♔xg5 ♔b4 17 h6 a4 18 h7 a3 19 h8♕ 1-0

This next example is a rook endgame in which White starts out with an extra pawn and his rook powerful placed on the seventh rank, but the position gets away from him because he becomes too materialistic. Black, on the other hand, advances his queenside pawns with great resolve and soon has White on the defensive. It's no accident that chess writers throughout history have declared that passed pawns should be pushed, but it's hard to find such a vivid example of why at Grandmaster level.

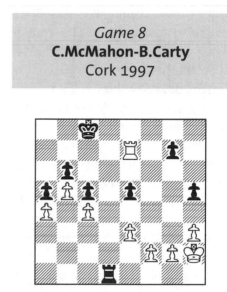

1 ♖xe5?

This is not the right idea. White is thinking in terms of material gain and thus captures one pawn while taking aim at another one on h5. But he should have been thinking in terms of creating a passed pawn on the kingside as quickly as possible.

The right way to play it was with 1 ♖xg7; for example, 1...♖a1 2 g4 h4 (or 2...hxg4 3 h4 ♖xa4 4 h5 with a coronation in the offing) 3 g5 ♔d8 4 g6 ♔e8 5 ♖b7 ♔f8 (if 5...♖xa4, 6 g7 goes through

to queen) 6 ♖xb6 ♖xa4 7 ♖b7 ♖xc4 8
♖f7+ ♔g8 9 b6 ♖b4 10 b7 a4 11 ♖c7 a3
12 ♖c8+ ♔g7 13 b8♕ etc.

1...♖a1! 2 ♖xh5 ♖xa4

Suddenly Black has counterplay
thanks to his passed a-pawn, and
White now panics.

3 ♖d5?

A typical mistake in rook endings;
White intends to defend against Black's
advancing queenside pawns with his
rook, but rooks are cut out for attack
rather than defence.

He should have played 3 ♖g5, when
3...♖xc4 4 ♖xg7 ♔b8 (Black has to play
this sooner or later because 4...a4 5 g4
a3 is met by 6 ♖a7!, getting the rook
behind Black's passed a-pawn) 5 g4 a4
6 g5 a3 7 g6 a2 8 ♖e7 (another possibility is to enter a queen ending with 8
♖g8+ ♔b7 9 ♖b8+ ♔xb8 10 g7 a1♕ 11
g8♕+ ♔a7 12 ♕xc4, but then 12...♕b2
intending 13...♕b4 could be tricky)
8...a1♕ 9 g7 ♕xg7 10 ♖xg7 should still
be winning for White.

3...♖xc4 4 f4 a4!

![chess diagram]

Unlike his opponent Black charges

his passed pawns down the board. And
soon there will be three of them.

5 ♖d3 ♖b4 6 ♖a3 c4 7 ♖c3

It's now too late to make a race of it.
After 7 g4 ♖xb5 8 ♖xa4 ♖c5 9 ♖a2 c3 10
♖c2 b5 11 ♔g3 b4 12 ♔f3 b3 Black wins
easily.

7...♔d7 8 ♖c2 ♖xb5 9 ♖xc4 ♖a5

Putting rooks *behind* passed pawns
is an important endgame principle of
immense practical value. Black's pur-
poseful and decisive play boils down to
knowing this idea.

**10 e4 a3 11 ♖d4+ ♔c6 12 ♖d1 a2 13
♔g3 b5! 14 ♔g4 b4 15 ♔f3 b3 0-1**

A superb illustration of the value of
endgame knowledge.

Moving to a deeper level, endgames
also help with middlegame play via
subtle psychological effects. If someone
is more confident in their endgame
ability they won't feel the same need to
obtain a huge material advantage or
mating attack. This in turn means they
will be less likely to force the position
or play for complications, instead al-

lowing the position to unfold naturally. I've worked with a number of people who have found endgames very useful in this regard, one of them being Mark Josse...

Case History: Mark Josse

Mark consulted me in 2005 when he came back from a long break from chess and was playing to around 1800 level. It was evident that he had a gift for the game, especially with regard to his chess vision and feel for the attack. Yet, while his overall game was uncultivated, this talent had led him towards trying to attack or force matters even when the position didn't warrant it.

Here are four examples of his games, the first two indicating the relevant issues and the second two showing how successfully he managed to address them. The first game is a fairly direct illustration of how a weakness in the endgame can hobble results, with Black losing a position which should have been drawn.

> ### Game 9
> ### J.Orjakhel-M.Josse
> ### Thames Valley League 2005
> *Pirc Defence*

1 e4 d6 2 ♘f3 g6 3 ♗c4 ♗g7 4 d4 ♘f6

In my book on the Modern Defence I advocated closing down the bishop on c4 with 4...e6.

5 ♘c3 0-0 6 0-0 ♗g4 7 h3 ♗xf3 8 ♕xf3

♘c6

9 ♘e2

A much more natural move is 9 ♗e3, which is in fact theory. Even so Black gets comfortable equality with 9...♘d7 10 ♖ad1 e5, for example 11 ♘e2 (11 dxe5 ♘cxe5 12 ♕e2 ♘xc4 13 ♕xc4 ♘b6 14 ♕b3 ♕f6 15 ♗d4 ♕e6 was OK for Black at this stage in R.Kholmov-E.Gufeld, USSR Team Championship 1966) 11...♕e7 12 c3 exd4 13 cxd4 ♘de5! 14 dxe5 ♘xe5 15 ♗xf7+ ♖xf7 16 ♕g3 ♘c4 17 b3 ♘xe3 18 ♕xe3 a5, as in R.Romanovsky-E.Gufeld, Ukrainian Championship, Kiev 1963.

9...♘d7 10 c3 e5

It was already worth considering 10...♘ce5, though 11 dxe5 ♘xe5 12 ♗xf7+ ♖xf7 13 ♕e3, followed by 14 f4, would have given White a useful space advantage.

11 ♗e3 exd4 12 cxd4

After 12 ♘xd4 Black gets the initiative with 12...♘ce5 13 ♕e2 ♘xc4 14 ♕xc4 ♖e8, making it awkward for White to defend the e4-pawn.

12...♘de5! 13 dxe5 ♘xe5 14 ♗xf7+

♖xf7 15 ♕g3 ♕e8?!

15...♘c4! looks stronger, when White has some problems. After the move played he is slightly better.

16 ♗d4 ♘c6 17 ♗xg7 ♔xg7 18 ♘c3

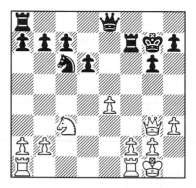

White is better here because of his central pawns and the exposed black king.

18...♘d4?!

This looks rather artificial. Black should have completed his development with 18...♕e6 19 f4 ♖af8 when his position is OK, although I prefer White.

19 ♖ad1 ♕e5

20 ♕xe5+?!

Giving away the advantage. He should play 20 f4 ♕c5 21 ♔h1 with the better game.

20...dxe5 21 f4 ♘c6 22 fxe5 ♖xf1+ 23 ♔xf1 ♘xe5

Black is doing quite well now thanks to his strongly-placed knight on e5 and queenside pawn majority. But after the middlegame the Gods placed the ending.

24 b3 c6 25 ♔e2 ♔f6 26 ♔e3 ♔e6 27 ♘a4 b6 28 ♘c3 ♖f8 29 ♘e2 ♔e7 30 ♘g1 ♔e6 31 ♘f3 ♘xf3 32 gxf3 g5

This shouldn't lose but it saddles Black with more responsibilities than he needs. Black's pawn majority is on the queenside so he should set about using it with 32...c5 33 f4 ♖c8.

33 a4?!

I don't really understand this move. The immediate 33 ♖g1 looks better, after which 33...h6 34 h4 is good for White.

33...h6

Black can hold the position with 33...♖f6 34 ♖g1 ♖g6.

34 h4

34...罝b8?

And after this he is in serious trouble. 34...gxh4 was mandatory, when 35 罝h1 h5 36 罝xh4 罝h8 37 f4 c5 seems to offer adequate counterplay.

35 hxg5 hxg5 36 罝h1 堂d6 37 b4 c5 38 罝h6+ 堂e5

Or 38...堂e7 39 bxc5 bxc5 40 罝h7+ 堂e6 41 罝xa7 etc.

39 罝g6 c4

Perhaps 39...cxb4 might have been a better try, though 40 罝xg5+ 堂e6 41 罝b5 looks good then.

40 罝xg5+ 堂e6 41 堂d4 罝c8 42 堂c3 罝c7 43 f4 罝f7 44 罝g6+ 堂d7 45 f5 罝e7 46 罝g4 堂d6 47 堂xc4 堂e5

48 堂d3

48 罝g6 would have been quicker.

48...罝d7+ 49 堂e3 罝d4 50 f6 罝d7 51 罝f4 罝f7 52 罝f5+ 堂e6 53 堂d4 罝d7+ 54 堂c4 堂f7 55 e5 a6 56 罝g5 罝c7+ 57 堂d4 罝c1 58 罝g7+ 堂f8 59 罝b7 罝d1+ 60 堂e4 1-0

This next game shows how the pressure of playing for complications can take its toll, White's 11 b4 in particular being symptomatic of a player who feels he must force things at every moment.

Game 10
M.Josse-A.Ashby
Civil Service League 2005
French Defence

---

1 e4 e6 2 d4

An interesting line for aggressive players is a gambit with 2 ⒩f3 d5 3 e5 c5 4 b4!? cxb4 5 d4, when White's centre is secure and Black's king will have trouble finding long-term safety.

2...d5 3 ⒩c3

And here 3 exd5 might be considered in order to get a more open position. It's not as drawish as its reputation suggests and, indeed, Kasparov himself played it after having some trouble with the French.

3...堂b4 4 堂d2

This is not a bad line by any means and Black comes up with a dubious response. But the tendency to play for complications from the outset is not a particularly positive sign for players who want to improve rather than have fun. Mark would later switch to the Tarrasch Variation with 3 ♘d2, notching up some impressive results.

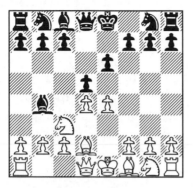

4...♘f6 5 e5 ♘fd7 6 ♕g4 ♔f8 7 a3

This position should be very good for White, but from the following moves it's clear that it's not his cup of tea. I quite like 7 0-0-0, with rapid development.

7...♗e7 8 f4 c5

8...f5 is worth considering, but looks good for White after 9 ♕h3 intending g2-g4.

9 ♘f3 ♘c6 10 dxc5 ♘xc5

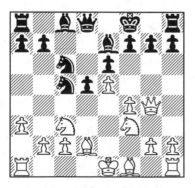

11 b4?!

Forcing the position for the sake of it. I don't like this move at all, as White drives the knight to a good square and creates targets on the queenside. 11 0-0-0 looks much better.

11...♘e4 12 ♗d3 ♘xd2

Although White's dark-squared bishop appears to be 'bad' (it is shut in by his own pawns) it helps cover important squares.

13 ♘xd2 ♕b6 14 ♘b3?

14 ♘e2 is better, with approximate equality. Now it's Black who gets to attack.

14...♘xb4! 15 axb4 ♗xb4 16 ♔e2 ♗xc3 17 ♖ab1 ♕c7 18 h4 a5 19 ♖h3 a4 20 ♖g3 f5 21 exf6 ♗xf6 22 ♘d2

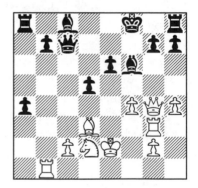

22 ♘a1 e5 is also the end of the road for White.

22...e5 23 ♗f5 exf4 24 ♖d3 ♕e5+ 0-1

Let's look now at two more recent games which show a complete transformation. In the first one Mark sacrifices a pawn, but then sees that the logical way to exploit his advantage is by exchanging queens (18 ♕c7!). This shows remarkable growth and discipline, and stems from knowing that checkmate in the middlegame is not the only way to win.

1 e4 e6 2 d4 d5 3 ♘d2

A sign of an evolving style of play. Rather than the tricky 3 ♘c3 ♗b4 4 ♗d2 variation, Mark now chooses a serious main line.

3...♘f6 4 e5 ♘fd7 5 ♗d3 c5 6 c3 ♘c6 7 ♘gf3

And here's where the sharpness comes in; he's not afraid to offer a pawn sacrifice which playing this line involves. 7 ♘e2 is the main line, leaving f3 for the knight on d2 so as to lend protection to the d4-pawn.

7...♕b6 8 0-0 cxd4 9 cxd4 ♘xd4 10 ♘xd4 ♕xd4 11 ♘f3 ♕b6 12 ♕a4 ♗e7

13 a3

Mark had previously played 13 ♗e3 in this position, but now he varies after a long thought. In any case White has excellent positional compensation for the pawn because of his space, lead in development, and control of the c-file and d4-square.

13...0-0 14 ♕c2 g6

This makes it very difficult for Black to move his f-pawn in future, so he basically condemns himself to passivity. After 14...f5 White should probably take en passant, though the continuation 15 exf6 ♘xf6 16 ♗e3 ♕c6 looks OK for Black.

15 b4 ♕d8 16 ♗e3 b6

This creates more weaknesses, but it's already getting difficult to see what Black can do.

17 ♖fc1 ♗b7 18 ♕c7!

Rightly seeing that this is the logical move, despite the fact that it will entail the exchange of queens. A few years earlier I doubt Mark would have played this way.

18...♕c8 19 ♗b5 ♖d8 20 ♘d4 a6

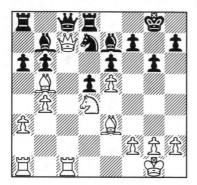

21 ♗a4

Mark rejected the line 21 ♕xc8 ♖axc8 22 ♗c6 because he saw Black hanging on after 22...♖b8 23 ♗xb7 ♖xb7 24 ♘c6 ♖e8 25 ♘xe7+ ♖xe7 26 ♖c8+ ♔g7. So the forcing line is rejected in favour of keeping up the pressure.

21...b5 22 ♗b3

22 ♗d1 looks as if it might be stronger, as from e2 it can hit b5. In any case White has strong pressure.

22...♕xc7 23 ♖xc7

White has lots for the pawn even in the endgame. In fact in many ways the endgame allows him better access to Black's weaknesses.

23...♖ab8 24 ♖ac1 ♔f8 25 f4 ♔e8 26 ♔f2!

A good positional move with a drop of poison.

26...♖dc8?

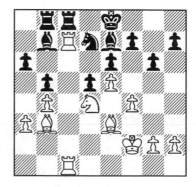

Missing the point of White's last move. Now the game is decided.

27 ♖xb7! ♖xc1 28 ♖xb8+ ♘xb8 29 ♗xc1 ♔d7

Black could really have saved himself the rest.

30 ♔e2 ♘c6 31 ♔d3 ♘xd4 32 ♔xd4 ♔c6 33 ♗d2 ♗d8 34 ♔d3 ♗b6 35 ♗e3 ♗xe3 36 ♔xe3 ♔b6 37 ♔d4 ♔c6 38 g4 ♔b6 39 ♗c2 h6 40 h3 ♔c6 41 h4 ♔b6 42 ♗d3 ♔c6 43 h5 gxh5 44 gxh5 ♔b6 45 ♗g6 1-0

The final game is a classy demolition of the experienced McDonald-Ross, this time showing other aspects of Mark's game, in that he weakened Black's pawn structure and then allowed his opponent some play in the vicinity of his king, knowing full well that it was not enough. This skill and confidence stems from the broader outlook that endgame study helps cultivate.

1 e4 c5 2 ♘c3 ♘c6 3 ♗b5

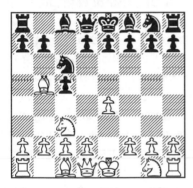

This is quite a nice line, not least because Black is still having trouble figuring out what to do about it.

3...e6 4 ♗xc6 bxc6 5 d3 d6

Black should probably play 5...d5, followed by 6...♘f6. He can defend the c5-pawn well enough.

6 f4 ♕h4+ 7 g3 ♕d8 8 ♘f3 ♗e7 9 ♕e2 ♘h6

Trying to avoid the mangling of his pawns after 9...♘f6 10 e5, but 9...d5 and 10...♘f6 may be a better way to do it. Of course this would mean admitting that 5...d6 was not the best, which isn't easy for people to do.

10 ♗d2 0-0 11 b3 f5

Ruling out f4-f5 by White, but the real problem lies with his doubled c-pawns.

12 0-0 ♖e8 13 ♘a4 ♘f7 14 ♖ad1 ♗f8 15 ♕f2

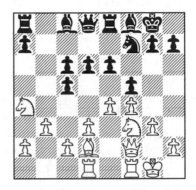

With the knight on f7, rather than d7, that c5-pawn is a real problem.

15...e5 16 fxe5 fxe4 17 dxe4 ♗h3

17...♘xe5?? 18 ♘xe5 dxe5 19 ♕f7+ ♔h8 20 ♗g5 would win on the spot.

18 ♖fe1 ♘xe5 19 ♘xe5 ♖xe5 20 ♗f4 ♖h5 21 ♕e2 ♕e8

Perhaps 21...g6 was better, though this is very nice for White after 22 ♗xd6 ♗xd6 23 ♕c4+ ♔g7 24 e5 etc.

22 ♗xd6 ♕g6 23 e5 ♗g4?!

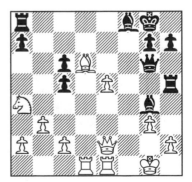

Or if 23...♖e8 there follows 24 ♘xc5 ♗xd6 25 ♕c4+ ♕f7 26 ♕xf7+ ♔xf7 27 ♖xd6 ♖hxe5 28 ♖xe5 ♖xe5 29 ♘d3 etc. **24 ♕c4+ ♔h8 25 ♖d2 ♕h6 26 ♖f2 ♗e6 27 ♕xc5 ♖f5 28 ♖xf5 ♗xf5 29 ♗xf8 ♕d2 30 ♕f2 ♕xf2+ 31 ♔xf2 ♖xf8 32 ♔e3 ♗xc2 33 ♖c1 ♗f5 34 ♖xc6 ♖e8 1-0**

A very clear and convincing game on White's part.

At the time of writing Mark Josse has improved to around 2200 and started to claim scalps amongst titled players. He has the potential to develop further still, showing that adult players can indeed improve and that the endgame is a wonderful tool with which to bring this about.

Key Points

1. Endgame study is usually neglected by players who wish to improve but represents a wonderful opportunity to pile on the rating points. Look out for endgame books that you find to be readable (many of the older books fall into this category) and do a little every day.

2. For players who seem to have reached the upper limit of their tactical ability (continued practice is no longer producing dividends) the endgame is the way to go. Being more knowledge-based in nature, endgame skill can be developed by dedication alone and without particular talent.

3. Players with considerable tactical strength can also benefit greatly from studying the endgame. In cases where they become over-reliant on tactics, to the extent that it scuppers their objectivity with various opening and middlegame decisions, the endgame can lead to considerable growth by offering an alternative way of winning games.

4. For beginners the endgame offers a highly effective way of improving their game, because it allows them to explore and understand the powers of the individual pieces. A board full of pieces will not allow them to do this in the same way.

Chapter Three

Keep Company with the Strong

"As water changes according to the soil through which it flows, so a man assimilates the character of his associates." – Saint Tiruvalluvar (*The Holy Kural*, verse 452)

One of the very best ways to improve your chess is to increase the strength of your peer group. By hanging out with people who are good at what they do you can gradually acquire their understanding and attitudes. All too often you see birds of a feather flocking together and comforting themselves with their shared resentment of people more skilled than themselves.

How should someone go about this? Well, one way is to join a chess club in which there are stronger players and listen to what they have to say. Another way is to find a teacher and get him or her to monitor your development as a player. Having an expert eye cast over your games can make all the difference, allowing flaws to be discovered light years before you can divine the problem for yourself.

It really amazes me that so many chess players seem willing to undergo years of frustration and thousands of hours ineffective training rather than enlist the help of an expert. Although books and DVDs have their place, they do not point out what players are doing wrong.

Case History: Nigel Davies

It was in the little town of Protvino in 1988 that I learned about this improvement method. As was traditional for tournaments in Russia, the Westerners were getting badly beaten and seemed to exude a sense of gloomy resignation. Curiously I managed to stay immune from its effects, and I believe this was because of spending many hours in conversation with the Russian participants and visiting dignitaries such as David Bronstein and Mark Dvoretsky. I had the best result of all the Western players, finishing midway with 50%.

A couple of years later I went to live in Israel at the time when many strong players were emigrating from Russia. I was soon to find myself in a team which comprised Grandmasters Lev Psakhis, Ilya Smirin and Vladimir Liberzon, plus several strong International Masters, and usually I was sandwiched between Smirin and Liberzon on board 3. I also became good friends with Psakhis, and as we lived in the same town I used to visit him quite regularly. Although the visits were primarily social, when Lev talked about chess I listened; he often showed me his games and I started experimenting with some of the opening systems he used.

The next few years of living in 'little Russia' started a profound change in my understanding of chess. From being a self-taught International Master who spent most of his time as Black on three rows (when I arrived in Israel I played the Modern Defence almost exclusively) I started playing more like my new compatriots. And then in 1993 a breakthrough came and I made the remaining two GM norms I needed for the title, plus some other good results. I was playing at around 2570 strength that year, up from the 2460 or so of my

International Master days.

The following games are graphic examples of the way my game changed during these years. The first two feature your hapless author being crushed in the Modern during a period in which I had downright poor results against 1 e4. The second two feature games I played with 1...e5, where my results in terms of Elo rating were over 100 points better than with the Modern.

Game 13
Art.Minasian-N.Davies
Lyon Open 1990
Modern Defence

1 e4 g6 2 d4 ♗g7 3 ♘c3 d6 4 ♗g5 ♘c6

This provocative move featured heavily in my interpretation of the Modern, my other main plan being an expansion on the queenside with ...a7-a6, ...b7-b5, ...♘d7 and ...c7-c5. In either case White is, of course, being handed a large lead in development.

5 d5 ♘e5 6 f4 ♘d7 7 ♘f3 c6 8 ♕d2 cxd5

9 exd5 ♘gf6 10 0-0-0 ♘c5 11 ♘d4 ♘fe4

After the game I thought that 11...♗d7 12 ♖e1 ♖c8 would have been a good idea, with Minasian then suggesting 13 f5!?. In fact the text is also quite playable if Black follows it up correctly.

12 ♘xe4 ♘xe4 13 ♕e3 ♘xg5 14 fxg5 14 fxg5 0-0

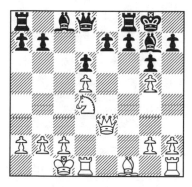

This should not be too bad for Black, because now White lacks an easy means of exchanging off Black's dark-squared bishop on the kingside.

15 ♗c4 ♗d7

Fritz likes 15...♗g4 16 ♖d2 ♕b6 for Black, which stops White's queen's rook coming to the h-file, while developing Black's pieces. Actually it looks quite good.

16 h4 b5?!

And here 16...♖c8 was the right move; for example, 17 ♗b3 a5 18 a4 ♗e5 19 h5?! ♗g4 20 hxg6 fxg6 with White suddenly finding himself in serious trouble. My moves look like I was going through the motions rather than buzzing along in top form, and this can

be fatal in the Modern.

17 ♗e2 ♖c8 18 h5 ♖c5?

18...♗e5 19 hxg6 fxg6! was the right idea, while Black meets 19 ♘f3 with 19...♕b6 in order to bail out into an endgame.

19 hxg6 hxg6 20 ♕e4 ♕c7?

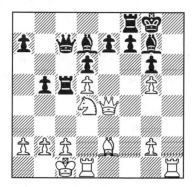

The fatal mistake. 20...e5 would have kept me on the board; for example, 21 dxe6 (or 21 ♕h4 ♖e8) 21...♕xg5+ 22 ♔b1 ♖e5 23 ♕b7 ♗xe6 and Black is OK.

21 ♗d3 ♖c8?

21...♕b7 is better, though White has a strong attack after 22 ♕h4.

22 ♖df1 ♖c4

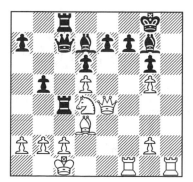

23 ♖xf7! 1-0

White has a winning attack; for example, 23...♔xf7 (or 23...♖xd4 24 ♕xg6 etc) 24 ♕xg6+ ♔g8 25 ♕h7+ ♔f8 26 ♖f1+ ♔e8 27 ♕g8+ followed by mate.

The reader will probably understand why this game did not appear in my book on the Modern! It was one of my worst defeats with this opening and I thought that people might be scared into never playing this opening once they had seen the author getting beaten so badly. Actually there are improvements for Black throughout the game, but it takes a lot of nervous energy to play this way. I now take the view that the Modern Defence should be used rather sparingly because of this, with openings that are easier to play forming the backbone of a player's repertoire.

> ### Game 14
> ### D.Velimirovic-N.Davies
> Vrnjacka Banja 1991
> *Modern Defence*

1 e4 d6 2 d4 g6

My favourite defence at the time, though this is undoubtedly a risky way to play against such an aggressive opponent as Velimirovic.

3 ♘c3 ♗g7 4 f4 ♘c6 5 ♗b5

This is the reason I later started setting up my hippopotamus formation with 4...e6, followed by ...♘e7, ...♘d7, ...a7-a6, ...b7-b6 and ...♗b7. After White

takes on c6 I find it difficult to get counterplay. Of course none of this is particularly appropriate against a ferocious attacking player like Velimirovic, who needs to be shut down as soon as possible.

5...a6 6 ♗xc6+ bxc6 7 ♘f3 f5?!

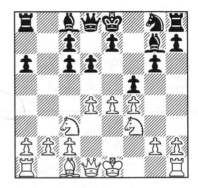

This seemed like a good idea at the time, but White's reply condemns my favourite bishop on g7 to passivity. Given this position again – and I wouldn't particularly want to have it again unless threatened with the loss of a fingernail – I'd probably play 7...♘f6.

8 e5 ♘h6 9 ♕e2 e6 10 ♗e3 0-0 11 0-0-0 ♗d7 12 h3 ♕b8

Aiming for counterplay along the b-file, but without the aid of my bishop on g7 this is essentially doomed to failure.

13 g4 ♕b4

Fritz merrily recommends 13...fxg4 14 hxg4 ♘xg4 at this point, seeing that it wins a pawn. Unfortunately White can meet this with 15 ♖xh7!; for example, 15...♘xe3 (or 15...♔xh7 16 ♘g5+

♔g8 17 ♕xg4 with a massive attack) 16 ♖dh1 ♘f5 17 ♘g5 ♘g3 18 ♕d3 ♘xh1 19 ♕xg6 ♖f7 20 ♖h8+ ♔xh8 21 ♕h7 mate.

14 a3 ♕b7 15 g5 ♘f7 16 h4 ♖fb8 17 b3 c5

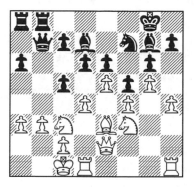

The only way to get some kind of counterplay, but it also helps get White's pieces working.

18 h5 cxd4 19 hxg6 hxg6 20 ♘xd4

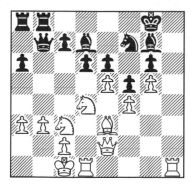

20...c5

At first *Fritz* does not see a problem for Black with 20...dxe5 21 ♘xf5 gxf5 22 g6 ♘d6, but then starts to change its mind after 23 fxe5. Of course White has a huge attack for his sacrificed

piece, but *Fritz* will weigh just the material until it sees something clear.

21 ♘xf5! exf5 22 ♕h2 ♗c6 23 ♕h7+ ♔f8 24 ♖h2 ♕e7

Here, too, *Fritz* weighs in with 24...♗f3, but given 25 ♕xg6 ♗xd1 26 ♘xd1 c4 27 e6 cxb3 and then 28 ♗d4!, decides that it is also good for White.

25 ♕xg6 ♖d8 26 e6 ♗xc3

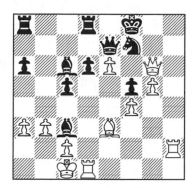

Losing quickly, but at this stage I did not particularly mind.

27 ♖h7 ♗e8 28 ♖dh1 ♖a7 29 ♗d2 ♗d4 30 c3 ♘h6 31 ♕xh6+ 1-0

Game 15
M.Kaminski-N.Davies
Liechtenstein Open 1993
Ruy Lopez

1 e4 e5

Probably the best medicine after years of playing the Modern Defence. Black immediately stakes out territory in the centre of the board and will develop his pieces quickly.

2 ♘f3 ♘c6 3 ♗b5 a6 4 ♗a4 ♘f6 5 0-0

♗e7 6 ♕e2

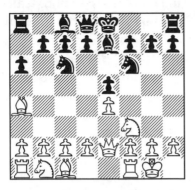

The other benefit of switching openings can be surprise. Kaminski might have been tempted to play this unusual line after having expected a Modern and assuming that my 1...e5 knowledge might not extend to sidelines. But I have played this way myself in a number of games.

6...b5 7 ♗b3 0-0 8 c3 d6 9 ♖d1

This is one of the points behind putting the queen on e2: White's rook can come to the d-file. The drawback is that it's rather slow and Black can obtain a satisfactory position quite easily.

9...♘a5 10 ♗c2 c5 11 d4 ♕c7

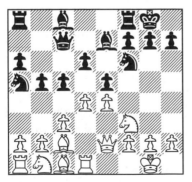

12 dxe5

White has other moves here, though without making much of an impact:

a) 12 ♗g5 ♗g4 13 dxe5 dxe5 14 ♘bd2 ♖fd8 (the immediate 14...♘h5 also seems fine) 15 ♘f1 ♘h5 16 h3 ♗e6 (16...♗xf3 17 ♕xf3 ♗xg5 18 ♕xh5 ♕e7 is also very comfortable for Black) 17 ♘e3 f6 18 ♘h2 was A.Alekhine-P.Keres, Salzburg 1942, and now Keres may have rejected 18...♗f7 because of 19 ♘d5!? ♖xd5 20 exd5 fxg5 21 ♗xh7+ ♔xh7 22 d6, but Black is better after 22...♕b7 23 dxe7 ♘f4 24 ♕g4 ♕xe7.

b) 12 h3 cxd4 (12...♗d7 may be more circumspect, waiting for White to develop his queen's knight to d2 before playing ...c5xd4) 13 cxd4 ♗d7 14 dxe5 dxe5 15 ♘c3 ♖ac8 16 ♗b1 ♗e6 17 ♗g5 (17 ♘d5!?) 17...♖fd8 18 ♗d3 h6 19 ♗xf6 ♗xf6 20 ♘d5 ♗xd5 21 exd5 g6 and the position was about equal in R.Fine-S.Reshevsky, Syracuse 1934.

c) 12 d5 is the main move here, but closing the centre gives Black opportunities for counterplay based on ...c5-c4 and ...♘a5-b7-c5 and/or ...f7-f5.

S.Conquest-E.Bacrot, French Team Championship 1997, provided a good illustration of these themes, continuing 12...♗d7 13 ♘bd2 ♘h5 14 ♘f1 g6 15 g3 ♘c4 16 h4 ♘g7 17 b3 ♘b6 18 ♗h6 c4 19 b4 a5 20 a3 ♖a6 21 h5 axb4 22 axb4 ♖fa8 23 ♖xa6 ♖xa6 24 hxg6 hxg6 25 ♔g2 ♕a7 26 ♗c1 ♖a2 27 ♘e3 f5! with a large advantage for Black.

12...dxe5 13 ♘bd2 ♖d8

A couple of great specialists in the Black side of the Spanish have played 13...♗e6 here; for example, 14 ♘f1 ♖ad8 (14...♖fd8 15 ♖xd8+ ♖xd8 16 b3 ♘c6 17 ♘e3 h6 18 h3 ♗f8 19 ♗d2 ♕b7 20 c4 ♘d4 21 ♘xd4 cxd4 22 ♘d5 bxc4 23 bxc4 ♘d7 was good for Black in K.Tsiknopoulos-P.Keres, Helsinki Olympiad 1952) 15 ♗g5 ♖xd1 16 ♕xd1 ♘c4 17 ♕c1 ♖d8 18 b3 ♘b6 19 ♘e3 a5 20 a4 bxa4 21 bxa4 ♘c4 22 ♖b1 ♘xe3 23 ♗xe3 ♘d7 and Black was very comfortable in M.Filip-S.Gligoric, Helsinki Olympiad 1952.

14 ♘f1 ♖xd1 15 ♗xd1 ♗b7

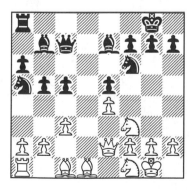

Black could also have played 15...♗e6, but I wanted to take aim at White's e4-pawn.

16 ♗c2 c4 17 ♘g3 g6 18 ♗g5 ♘c6 19 ♘d2 ♘h5

Black is already better here.

20 ♗xe7 ♘f4! 21 ♕f3

21 ♕e3 might have improved, when 21...♘xe7 22 ♘e2 ♘e6 is only slightly better for Black.

21...♘xe7 22 ♘e2?

And here White had to play something else, such as 22 ♘df1.

22...♖d8 23 ♕e3

After the text Black has a winning combination, but White is in trouble in any case. For example, 23 ♖d1 is simply met by 23...♘d3 with a very unpleasant position for White.

23...♘xg2!

A surprising and deadly shot.

24 ♔xg2

After 24 ♕g5 Black has several strong lines, the most spectacular of which is 24...f6! 25 ♕h6 (25 ♕xg2 ♖xd2 26 ♗d1 ♕d6 is a killer) 25...♕d7 26 ♖d1 (or 26 ♘xc4 ♕g4! etc) 26...♘e1! 27 ♖xe1 ♕xd2 28 ♕xd2 ♖xd2 and Black wins.

24...♞f5!

The point behind Black's previous move.

25 ♕g5 h6 26 ♕f6 ♖xd2 0-1

1 e4 e5 2 ♞f3 ♞c6 3 ♗b5 a6 4 ♗a4 ♞f6 5 0-0 ♗e7 6 ♖e1 b5 7 ♗b3 d6 8 c3 0-0 9 h3 ♗e6

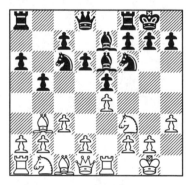

At the time I had a fondness for this old line. Despite the fact that 9...♗e6 is not particularly fashionable, it makes a lot of sense. Black develops a piece and is trying to exchange off the much-feared 'Spanish bishop' on b3.

10 d4 ♗xb3 11 axb3 exd4

I would later become somewhat disillusioned with this move, instead preferring to play 11...♕b8. But in that line Black admits to having the worst of it rather than attempting to gain equality.

12 cxd4 ♞b4

This makes perfect sense, advancing to the outpost in front of White's doubled b-pawns, though whether it equalizes or not is rather a moot point. If it doesn't, then Black should probably not take on d4 on his 11th move and instead strongpoint the e5-square.

13 d5

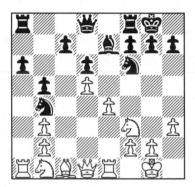

Attempting to cut across Black's plans. 13 ♞c3 is less challenging because of 13...c5.

13...c5 14 dxc6 d5

Again the most principled continuation. After 14...♞xc6 15 ♞c3 ♞e5 16 ♞d4 White's space advantage is a significant factor.

15 e5! ♞e4 16 ♞c3 ♞xc3

16...♞c5?! 17 ♗e3 ♞e6 18 ♖e2 was good for White in B.Zuckerman-P.Ostojic, Wijk aan Zee 1968.

17 bxc3 ♞xc6 18 ♕d3 ♖e8

The immediate 18...♕d7 is strongly met by 19 ♗g5!, when Black will struggle because of his weak pawns on d5 and a6.

19 e6!

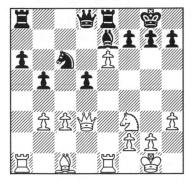

Still the right path, though it needs to be followed up accurately; White uses some time to loosen Black's king position. The main alternative is 19 ♗f4, but then 19...♕d7 gives Black a playable position; for example, 20 ♖ad1 ♖ad8 21 ♘g5 ♗xg5 22 ♗xg5 ♖c8 23 ♕xd5 ♕xd5 24 ♖xd5 f6 with equality.

19...fxe6 20 ♖xe6 ♕d7 21 ♖e2 b4

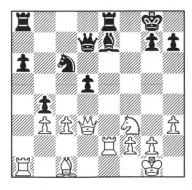

22 c4?!

This looks good but it is not the best. In the same tournament a year later Leonid Shmuter unveiled a significant improvement against me with 22 ♗b2!, and after 22...bxc3 (not

22...♗f6? because of 23 ♖xe8+ ♖xe8 24 ♖xa6) 23 ♗xc3 a5 24 ♘e5 ♘xe5 25 ♖xe5 d4 26 ♗xd4 I had lost a pawn for very little compensation (L.Shmuter-N.Davies, Rishon LeZion 1995).

22...♗f6 23 ♖aa2 d4 24 ♗g5 a5 25 ♗xf6 gxf6 26 ♘h4!?

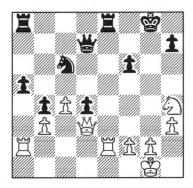

Sharp play by Gofshtein, trying to exploit the weakness of Black's king while allowing the d-pawn to run free. 26 ♖ed2 was a more pedestrian option.

26...♘e5 27 ♕g3+ ♔h8 28 ♕f4 d3! 29 ♖e4!?

Attempting to get the rook in front of the d-pawn, but this is very optimistic. On the other hand, winning a pawn via 29 ♕xf6+ does not seem much better; for example, 29...♕g7 30 ♕xg7+ ♔xg7 31 ♖ed2 a4! 32 f4? (32 ♖xa4 ♖xa4 33 bxa4 b3 34 ♘f5+ ♔g6 35 ♘e3 is more sensible, when White can probably draw) 32...axb3 33 ♖xa8 ♖xa8 34 fxe5 ♖a2 35 ♖xd3 ♖a1+ 36 ♔f2 b2 and White loses his rook.

29...♕c6 30 ♖d4

The logical follow-up, but the position is about to explode in White's face.

30 ♘f5 was probably better.
30...♖g8 31 ♔h2

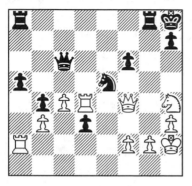

31...a4!

Creating a second and very dangerous passed pawn.

32 bxa4 ♖ad8 33 ♖d5 ♖de8 34 ♖d2 b3 35 ♘f3 ♘xc4

Giving up d3, as the pawn on b2 is about to get much stronger.

36 ♖2xd3 b2 37 ♖b5 ♘e5 38 ♖db3

As the b-pawn is finally rounded up, lightning now strikes on the other side of the board.

38...♖xg2+!! 39 ♔xg2 ♖g8+ 40 ♔h2 b1♕! 41 ♖xb1 ♘xf3+ 42 ♔h1 ♘d4+ 43 f3 ♘e2! 44 ♖b6

44 ♕e3 ♘g3+ 45 ♔h2 ♕c2+ 46 ♔g1 ♘f5+ wins White's queen.

44...♕xb6 45 ♖xb6 ♘xf4 46 ♖xf6 ♘h5

Black at last emerges a piece up, though it still requires accurate play. White might have drawn the game had his king not been so vulnerable or his pawns so weak.

47 ♖b6 ♖c8 48 a5 ♖c2 49 a6 ♖a2 50 ♔g1 ♘g3 51 ♖d6 ♔g7 52 ♖b6 h6 53 h4 ♘f5 54 h5 ♘d4 55 ♖g6+ ♔h7 56 ♖f6 ♔g7 57 ♖g6+ ♔h7 58 ♖f6 ♘e2+

59 ♔f1

59 ♔f2 ♘f4+ also wins the h5-pawn.

59...♘g3+ 60 ♔e1 ♘xh5 61 ♖d6 ♘g3 62 ♖d7+ ♔g6 63 a7 ♘f5 64 f4 h5 65

♖b7 h4 66 ♖b2 0-1

I count myself as being very fortunate to have had the opportunity to learn from Lev Psakhis, but I had to be open to it for this to happen. Since this time I have applied the same approach to other interests, seeking out the best mentors and teachers available.

Key Points

1. Do whatever you can to improve the strength of your peer group, whether this is through joining a chess club (or possibly a *stronger* chess club), attending stronger tournaments, moving to a major city, or seeking out a mentor.

2. When stronger players are playing or analysing together, pay close attention: there is much to be learned.

3. Seriously consider taking lessons; there's nothing like one-to-one tuition for developing strength in any field.

4. Avoid mixing with those who seem to resent stronger players while glorying in their own mediocrity.

Chapter Four

Take up Correspondence Chess

Correspondence chess is an excellent training tool, but one which is often misunderstood. When I suggest to people that this form of the game is a good way to improve, they often react by saying that everyone uses computers so what's the point? While this is not altogether true – there are correspondence chess players who agree to play without silicon assistance – I take the view that extensive use of computers is actually a good thing.

The point is that it vastly enhances the quality of your opponents' play, thus forcing you to raise your own level. So the faster their computer the better: it helps our training. Of course any ego damage caused by losing to these beasts must be put aside; the object of the exercise is to cultivate our chess game rather than score points.

The effect of having such a strong opponent is manifold. First of all you get the opportunity to play some main lines, rather than the anti-theory that usually occurs in club chess. The possibility of using *ChessBase* helps players get over their concerns that they do not know any theory: in correspondence chess they can simply look things up.

The other great effect is that you can no longer rely on the clock or tactical tricks to win; you need to outplay your opponent and his computer on a deep, strategic level. This provides an evolutionary incentive to play deeper and more correct chess, which will then spill over into over-the-board games.

Where should you play? The simplest solution is to sign up at one of the many online correspondence chess servers. I certainly would not suggest messing around with postcards and snail mail as they used to do in the past. Generally what happens is that you receive an email notification when one of your opponents has played a move, and you can then figure out what to do before you log on and reply.

Case History: Nigel Davies

Once again I have the best and most vivid examples of the benefits of correspondence chess in my own games. Figuring that I needed a new defence to the Ruy Lopez I decided to give a sharp variation of the Keres system a try in correspondence chess. During this time I learned a tremendous amount about it, in particular that the main exponent of this line, Alexander Graf (formerly Nenashev), did not play it particularly well! When I used his interpretation of this line, with 17...f5 against Butunoi and 15...b4 against Schulze, I got into all sorts of trouble. But these games did not really matter to me as I never saw correspondence play as anything but an opportunity to experiment and learn.

By the time I started using this system in over-the-board games all the wrinkles had been ironed out and it proved to be a highly effective weapon. Two of my best wins were against Jonathan Rowson and Adam Hunt.

> *Game 17*
> **A.Butunoi-N.Davies**
> Correspondence 2003
> *Ruy Lopez*

1 e4 e5 2 ♘f3 ♘c6 3 ♗b5 a6 4 ♗a4 ♘f6

5 0-0 ♗e7 6 ♖e1 b5 7 ♗b3 d6 8 c3 0-0 9 h3 ♘a5 10 ♗c2 c5 11 d4 ♘d7!?

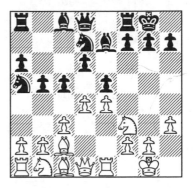

The move which characterizes the Keres variation. Prior to this 11...♕c7 had been thought to be more or less mandatory.

12 ♘bd2 exd4

And this, followed by 13...♘c6, is Graf's line. Black creates an asymmetrical pawn structure in which his queenside majority compensates for White's central pawn duo.

13 cxd4 ♘c6 14 d5 ♘ce5 15 ♘xe5 ♘xe5 16 f4 ♘g6 17 ♘f3 f5?

I played this move because Graf had done so, but it gets refuted in this game. Black should opt for 17...♗h4, after which 18 ♘xh4 ♕xh4 19 ♖f1 ♗xh3 20 gxh3 ♕g3+ leads to a draw by perpetual check.

18 e5 dxe5 19 fxe5 ♗b7 20 d6 ♗h4 21 ♖f1 ♗g3

An unusual and ingenious way of attacking the pawn on e5. Unfortunately for Black classical chess principles are about to be reasserted.

22 ♘g5

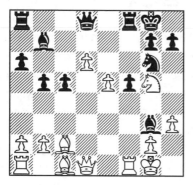

22...♕e8

The game I was following was O.Korneev-A.Graf, Jakarta 1997. This had gone 22...♘h4 23 ♕h5 h6 24 ♘e6 ♕b6 25 ♕e2 ♗xg2 with wild complications, and in reaching this position I had fully intended to follow this line. But then I saw that White had the incredibly strong 23 ♗e4!!, after which 23...fxe4 24 ♕b3+ and 25 ♕xg3 would be hopeless for Black. In desperation I came up with 22...♕e8, but it's not much better.

23 ♗xf5 ♕xe5

23...♖xf5 24 ♖xf5 ♗xe5 25 d7 is just as bad; for example, 25...♕e7 (25...♕b8

26 ♕h5) 26 ♖f7 ♗d4+ 27 ♔h1 ♕d8 28 ♕h5 etc.

24 ♗e6+ ♔h8 25 ♖xf8+ ♖xf8 26 d7 ♗h2+ 27 ♔h1 ♕g3

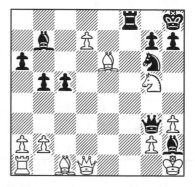

Obviously White will see through this shallow threat of mate, but I did not know what else I could do.

28 ♕e2 ♘e5 29 ♗d2 1-0

The position is quite hopeless for Black in view of White's passed d-pawn and the fact that the bishop on h2 cannot be extricated.

Game 18
M.Schulze-N.Davies
Correspondence 2003
Ruy Lopez

1 e4 e5 2 ♘f3 ♘c6 3 ♗b5 a6 4 ♗a4 ♘f6 5 0-0 ♗e7 6 ♖e1 b5 7 ♗b3 d6 8 c3 0-0 9 h3 ♘a5 10 ♗c2 c5 11 d4 ♘d7 12 ♘bd2 exd4 13 cxd4 ♘c6 14 d5 ♘ce5 15 a4

A more sophisticated treatment than Butunoi's 15 ♘xe5 ♘xe5 16 f4, but no less critical.

15...b4?

Once again following Graf's example rather too unquestioningly. 15...♖b8 is a better move, keeping control of c4.

16 ♘xe5 ♘xe5 17 f4 ♘g6 18 ♘c4 a5 19 e5!

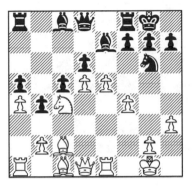

A huge improvement for White which effectively busts this line.

The game I was following featured 19 b3, when 19...♗a6 20 ♗d3 ♗f6 21 ♖a2 ♗d4+ 22 ♔h2 ♖a7 23 g3 f6 24 ♗e3 ♗c3 25 ♗d2 ♗d4 26 ♗e3 led to a draw by repetition in V.Iordachescu-A.Graf, European Championship, Istanbul 2003.

In another of my correspondence games (H.Bunyan-N.Davies, IECG World Championship semi-final 2003) White tried 19 f5!?, but this time Black was OK after 19...♗a6! 20 fxg6 ♗xc4 21 gxh7+ ♔h8 22 ♕g4 ♕c8! 23 ♕g3 ♕d8!, again inviting a draw by repetition (which White should have accepted).

19...♗b7

I also considered 19...dxe5 20 fxe5 ♗h4, but this looks bad for Black after 21 ♖e2 ♗a6 22 b3 ♗g3 23 ♗xg6 hxg6

24 ♕d3, keeping White's huge pawn centre.

20 ♕d3!

Another accurate move. I was hoping White would play 20 ♗e4, when I would have obtained some counterplay via 20...♗a6 21 b3 f5 22 ♗c2 ♗xc4 23 bxc4 ♗h4 24 ♖e2 ♗g3 attacking f4.

20...f6

The other move I looked at was 20...♖e8, but I couldn't see how I'd get my pawn back after 21 exd6 ♗f6 22 ♖xe8+ ♕xe8 23 ♕e4.

20...dxe5 is also bad because of 21 f5 b3 (or 21...e4 22 ♖xe4 ♕xd5 23 fxg6 ♕xe4 24 gxh7+ ♔h8 25 ♕xe4 ♗xe4 26 ♗xe4 etc) 22 ♗b1 ♕xd5 (22...e4 23 ♕xb3) 23 ♕xd5 ♗xd5 24 ♘b6 etc.

21 h4!

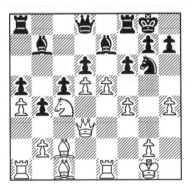

The threat of h4-h5 forces me to take desperate measures and I'm surprised I managed to scramble a draw. 21 e6 is strong, too, as Black would have to play 21...f5, leaving him with a very passive game.

21...b3 22 ♗b1

White could also play 22 ♕xb3; for

example, 22...♗xd5 23 h5 ♘h4 24 exd6 ♗xd6 25 ♕d3 etc.

22...fxe5

Both 22...dxe5 23 d6 and 22...♖e8 23 h5 ♘f8 24 exd6 were hopeless.

23 h5 ♗h4

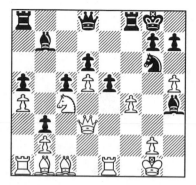

24 ♖e4?

A surprising error after White's previous excellent play. He has a strong line here in 24 ♖f1 ♖xf4 25 hxg6 ♖xf1+ 26 ♕xf1 and, frankly, I think Black is lost.

On the other hand, 24 ♖e2 can be met by 24...♖xf4 25 ♗xf4 ♘xf4 26 ♕xh7+ ♔f8, when it's still a fight.

24...♘xf4! 25 ♗xf4 ♖xf4 26 ♖xf4 exf4 27 ♕xh7+ ♔f8 28 ♗g6

After 28 ♕h8+ Black can calmly play 28...♔f7 29 ♗g6+ ♔f6 30 ♕h7 ♕h8 31 ♕xh8 ♖xh8 32 ♘xd6 ♗xd5 and, thanks to the two bishops, even stands better.

28...♕f6

Both kings are in trouble now!

29 ♖d1

I would have answered 29 h6 with 29...♗xd5, and 29 ♘b6 with 29...♗f2+ 30 ♔xf2 ♕xb2+ etc.

29...f3 30 h6 f2+ 31 ♔f1 ♗a6 32 ♕h8+ ½-½

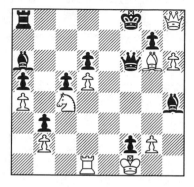

It will be a draw by perpetual check after 32...♔e7 33 ♕xa8 ♗xc4+ 34 ♗d3 ♕e5 35 ♕b7+ etc.

> ## Game 19
> ## A.Hunt-N.Davies
> Blackpool 2003
> *Ruy Lopez*

1 e4 e5 2 ♘f3 ♘c6 3 ♗b5 a6 4 ♗a4 ♘f6 5 0-0 ♗e7 6 ♖e1 b5 7 ♗b3 d6 8 c3 0-0 9 h3 ♘a5 10 ♗c2 c5 11 d4 ♘d7

This was the first game in which I tried the Keres system over the board and my opponent evidently expected something else. He played the first 11 moves confidently enough, but from move 12 onwards he started to consume lots of time.

12 d5!?

Although this is good in many lines of the Closed Spanish, in this particular position it is more controversial. The point is that Black is well prepared for

...f7-f5 here, having already moved his knight from f6. 12 d5 was used in a Fischer-Keres game, and although White can improve on Fischer's play, he needs to know exactly what he's doing.

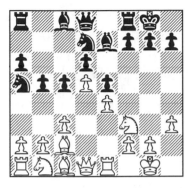

12...♘b6

Another interesting possibility is to transfer the knight on a5 to c4: 12...♘c4 13 b3 ♘cb6 14 a4 bxa4 15 bxa4 ♘c4 16 ♗d3 ♘a5 17 ♘a3 ♘b6 18 c4 ♘d7 gave Black a playable position in E.Sutovsky-P.Acs, Paks 2005.

13 b3

Not the best. R.J.Fischer-P.Keres, Candidates Tournament, Curacao 1962, featured the aggressive 13 g4, but this is not right either. After 13...h5 14 ♘h2 hxg4 15 hxg4 ♗g5 16 ♘d2 g6 Black already had the better game.

The correct move is 13 ♘bd2, which Peter Leko brought into the limelight in a couple of games against Kramnik and Adams. It used to be thought that 13...f5 was the right answer, but then 14 exf5 ♗xf5 15 ♗xf5 ♖xf5 16 ♘e4 has proven to be quite promising for White. In view of this it could be that

Black should play more slowly with 13...g6, though of course none of this is acutely relevant to our theme.

13...f5 14 exf5 ♗xf5 15 ♗xf5 ♖xf5 16 ♖e4?!

Perhaps White should have played 16 ♘a3, when 16...c4 could be met by 17 ♗e3, trying to undermine the support for Black's c4-pawn.

16...c4 17 b4 ♘b7

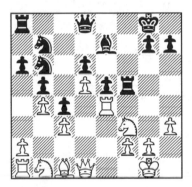

The knight is not very actively placed here, but White's d5-pawn is a much more serious problem. Cut off from its comrades it is a serious and permanent weakness.

18 ♘a3 ♕d7 19 g4?

Making a bad position much worse. White should try to defend himself rather than create additional weaknesses on the kingside.

19...♖f7 20 ♗e3 ♘a4

Knights are not always grim on the rim. This one will tie White's pieces down very effectively.

21 ♘b1

This miserable retreat is motivated by the need to defend the c3-pawn. But now White's position starts falling apart.

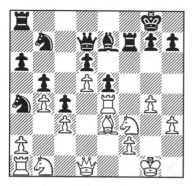

21...♖af8 22 ♘fd2 ♗d8

Bringing the bishop into play via b6.

23 a3 ♗b6 24 f3 ♘d8 25 ♔g2 ♕b7

More fire power against d5.

26 ♘f1 ♖xf3!

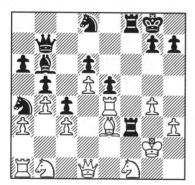

The decisive breakthrough. Although White gets two rooks for his queen, his pieces are too poorly coordinated to put up any resistance.

27 ♕xf3 ♖xf3 28 ♔xf3 ♕f7+

Forcing White's king to a worse square before taking the d5-pawn.

29 ♔e2 ♕xd5 30 ♘g3 ♕d3+ 31 ♔f2 ♕c2+ 0-1

Game 20
J.Rowson-N.Davies
British League 2004
Ruy Lopez

1 e4 e5 2 ♘f3 ♘c6 3 ♗b5 a6 4 ♗a4 ♘f6 5 0-0 ♗e7 6 ♖e1 b5 7 ♗b3 d6 8 c3 0-0 9 h3 ♘a5 10 ♗c2 c5 11 d4 ♘d7 12 ♘bd2 exd4 13 cxd4 ♘c6 14 d5 ♘ce5 15 a4

The same line that Schulze used against me; but having learned from that game, I play it a bit better this time.

15...♖b8

Improving on the correspondence game in which I played the mistaken 15...b4?!.

Another possibility is 15...♗b7, though I would be reluctant to put the bishop on a square where it bites on granite, in the shape of White's d5-pawn.

16 axb5 axb5 17 ♘h2

Rowson had evidently prepared for this game and comes up with a sophisticated and challenging treatment. By avoiding the exchange on e5 White hopes to show that Black has too many knights for the single e5-square.

In another of my games, M.Chandler-N.Davies, British League 2004, White tried 17 ♘b3, but without getting very far. After 17...♘xf3+ 18 ♕xf3 ♗f6 19 ♘a5 ♕b6 20 ♕g3 ♗b7 21 ♘xb7 ♖xb7 22 ♖a2 ♗e5 23 ♕g4 a draw was agreed in this rich position. Post game analysis indicated that Black certainly isn't worse.

17...♘g6 18 g3

Continuing his ambitious plan to deprive Black's knights of decent squares on the kingside. On the other hand, this does create weaknesses around his king – pawns cannot move backwards. The alternatives were not particularly troublesome for Black; for example, 18 ♘df3 ♖e8 and 18 ♘df1 ♗g5 give him comfortable play.

18...♘f6

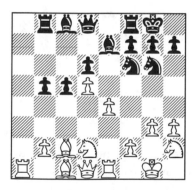

19 h4 h5

Preventing the further advance of White's h-pawn and gaining more of a grip on the g4-square. However, there's a case to be made for pure piece play; for example, 19...♖e8 20 f4 (20 h5 would be met by 20...♘e5) 20...♕d7!? intending ...♕h3 in some lines. This would lead to very complex play.

20 f4 ♘g4

Here, too, there were interesting alternatives in 20...♕d7 and 20...♖e8. Even now I don't know which move is the best, though in retrospect I don't particularly like my play in the game.

21 ♘df3 ♕b6 22 ♔g2 c4

This is the logical follow-up to 20...♘g4, but giving the d4-square away is very committal. I must admit to being influenced by the large amounts of time Rowson was taking over his moves and wanted to draw him ever deeper into time trouble.

23 ♕e2 b4!?

I felt this was necessary following my previous move. 23...♗f6 looks natural, but after 24 f5 ♘6e5 25 ♘xe5 ♗xe5 26 ♘xg4 hxg4 27 ♕xg4 Black's vulnerable king position is worrisome.

24 ♘d2

Running ever shorter of time, Rowson did not like the look of the line 24 ♘xg4 ♗xg4 (24...hxg4 25 ♘d2 is just good for White) 25 ♕xc4. For example, Black could try 25...b3!? 26 ♗e3 ♕d8 27 ♗xb3 ♗xf3+ 28 ♔xf3 ♕d7 with a lot of play for the pawns, though I'm not convinced this represents anything more than 'practical chances'; objectively speaking it may well be very good for White.

24...c3 25 bxc3 ♘xh2 26 ♔xh2 ♗g4 27 ♕e3 ♕d8!?

Still playing the position in a way that denies White safety and control. The best way may well be 27...♕xe3 28 ♖xe3 ♗f6, when Black could have just enough counterplay to offset his ragged pawns.

28 cxb4

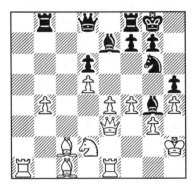

28...♗xh4!? 29 gxh4

White figures he might as well take the material, since if Black gets away with his bishop he can set White's kingside alight with ...h5-h4. A sample line is 29 ♘c4 ♗e7 30 ♗b2 h4 31 ♕c3 hxg3+ 32 ♕xg3 (32 ♔xg3 ♗f6 33 e5 ♗xe5! 34 fxe5 ♕h4+ 35 ♔g2 ♘f4+ gives

Black a winning attack) 32...♖xb4 33 ♕xg4 ♖xc4 34 ♗d3 ♖b4 35 ♖a2 ♗f6 with the position burning out to equality.

29...♕xh4+ 30 ♔g1 ♖fc8 31 ♖a2??

Missing a shot. White should have played 31 ♗d3, after which 31...♘xf4 32 ♗f1 holds the kingside together. Of course this would still be very difficult to play for White when down to his last few minutes.

31...♖c3!

The first of two hammer-blows which decide the game.

32 ♗d3

32 ♕xc3 ♕xe1+ 33 ♔h2 ♕f2+ 34 ♔h1 ♘xf4 would lead to mate.

32...♖xd3! 33 ♕xd3 ♕xe1+ 34 ♕f1 ♕g3+ 35 ♕g2 ♕xg2+ 36 ♔xg2 ♘xf4+ 37 ♔h2 ♖xb4

Black is winning thanks to his two extra pawns, though he has to be precise given the d6-weakness.

38 ♖c2 ♖a4 39 ♖c6

39 ♘c4 ♗d1 40 ♖b2 ♖xc4 41 ♗xf4 ♖xe4 42 ♗xd6 ♖d4 would win the last of White's pawns.

39...♘d3?!

39...♖a2 would have been even stronger, when 40 ♖xd6 ♘d3 wins a piece.

40 ♔g3 ♘xc1 41 ♖xc1 ♖d4 42 ♘c4 ♖xe4 43 ♘xd6 ♖d4

Putting the rook behind White's passed pawn.

44 ♖e1 ♖d3+ 45 ♔h2 f5 46 ♖e8+ ♔h7 47 ♘f7 ♖xd5 48 ♔g3 f4+!

A neat trick to get Black's pawns rolling. Capturing the pawn allows White's king and knight to be forked.

49 ♔h4 f3 50 ♘g5+ ♔g6 51 ♘e4 ♗d7 52 ♖e7 ♗f5 53 ♘f2 ♔f6 54 ♖a7 g5+ 55 ♔g3

After 55 ♔xh5 ♖d4 56 ♖a6+ ♗e6 White would have to give up his rook to stop the mate with 57...♖h4.

55...g4 56 ♔h4 ♖d2 57 ♖a6+ ♔e5 58 ♖a5+ ♔f4 0-1

Key Points

1. Correspondence chess can be a superb improvement tool if treated in the right way. The point is to use these games as training for your over-the-board chess rather than glorying in the results.

2. Play in events where computer use is not only allowed but encouraged! This is to get the strongest possible counters coming back at you.

3. Play openings which you would like to use in your over-the-board games, rather than have a separate repertoire. Be practical and realistic about your choices.

4. Avoid playing solely in correspondence events if you want to improve your over-the-board game. It is a very different discipline, with different habits involved in decision making. As such they need to be tempered by the practicalities of having to make quick moves in the hurly burly of a club or tournament.

Chapter Five

Create a Pre-Game Ritual

A little known but immensely powerful way of improving your results is to create a pre-game routine or ritual. This can have an instant impact on your results by triggering a state of mind in which you are ready to concentrate and fight.

Most strong players have a routine of some sort, whether or not they have formalized it into a conscious set of rules. David Bronstein once told me that he liked to take a walk of 20 minutes or so; other players may use anything from listening to favourite music to taking a nap. Such rituals may extend to arriving at the board a set amount of time before the game is due to begin, taking 'lucky pens' to the game, filling out the scoresheet in a particular way.

Although these habits may sometimes seem rather idiosyncratic, they serve a specific purpose. They are a sig-nal that a chess game is about to commence and that certain mental attributes need to be summoned.

What if players do not have a ritual and rush to the board to play their first moves without thinking or getting themselves 'set'? Well, here's a good example.

White arrived late to the game – as is so often the case for players who play after work – and without getting settled in, he finds it difficult to bring his concentration to bear...

Game 21
S.Healeas-N.Colter
London 2009
Queen's Pawn Opening

1 d4 e6 2 ♘f3

After the game White confessed

that he normally played his bishop out to f4 on his second move. Realizing his 'slip' he was determined to correct this as quickly as possible, doing so without regard for Black's reply.

2...c5 3 ♗f4?!

This is not a good idea in this precise position, and Black's reply points to the reason why. If White wants a London System he should play 3 c3 followed by 4 ♗f4.

3...♕b6!? 4 ♗c1?!

Flustered and still unsettled, White makes another poor move. There was a far more interesting possibility in 4 ♘c3, when 4...♕xb2 5 ♗d2 cxd4 (5...♘a6 is better) 6 ♖b1 dxc3 (6...♕a3 is bad because of 7 ♘b5) 7 ♖xb2 cxb2 8 ♗c3 wins Black's queen for inadequate compensation.

4...d5

I would have wanted to whittle away White's centre pawns with 4...cxd4, but the text is also pretty good.

5 e3 ♘f6 6 ♗e2 ♗d7 7 a4

Even now it looks like White has not settled in. It makes no sense to weaken the queenside like this.

7...♘c6 8 0-0 ♗d6 9 c3 0-0 10 ♘bd2 ♖fc8 11 a5 ♕c7

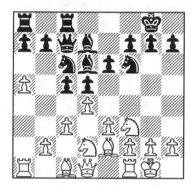

Not 11...♘xa5?! because of 12 dxc5 followed by 13 b4. But after the calm retreat of the queen, White's a-pawn becomes a long-term weakness.

12 a6 b6 13 ♗d3 c4

13...e5 is also quite good here.

14 ♗b1 ♘a5

I still like 14...e5 for Black.

Over the next few moves White has the opportunity to get back into the game with e3-e4, but when he lets this slip by he finds himself considerably worse.

15 ♕e2

He should have played 15 e4 dxe4 16 ♘xe4 ♘xe4 17 ♗xe4 ♗c6 18 ♕c2 ♗xe4 19 ♕xe4 ♘b3 20 ♖a2 intending 21 ♘g5, which sees White back in the game on more or less even terms. This is why Black should have played ...e6-e5 himself on moves 13 or 14.

15...♖ab8 16 h3 ♗c6 17 ♘g5

Here, too, 17 e4 was the right idea.

17...h6 18 ♘gf3 b5

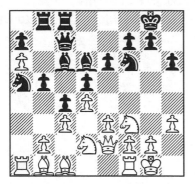

19 g4?

Missing the last chance for 19 e4 in favour of an ugly lurch forward on the kingside. The game now moves decisively in Black's favour.

19...g6

19...b4 is very strong.

20 ♘e5 ♗xe5 21 dxe5 ♘e4 22 ♗c2 ♗a8

And here 22...♘b3 would have been good, the point being that 23 ♗xb3 cxb3 24 ♘xb3 is answered by 24...b4! with various threats (such as 25...♗b5).

23 ♘xe4 dxe4 24 ♗d2 ♗d5

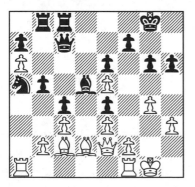

25 ♖a3?

Losing. White should have tried 25 ♕e1, when 25...♘c6 could be answered

by 26 f4! exf3? 27 e4!.

25...♘c6 26 b3?

Hastening his demise.

26...♘xe5 27 ♖fa1?! ♘f3+ 0-1

White never really got going in this game and I put it down to his lack of a pre-game ritual.

Over the years I've experimented quite a bit with what I do before a game and found an approach that works for me. As a player who tends to avoid critical opening theory there is not much need to prepare, but I do like to go in with a clear head. So, whenever possible, I take it easy the morning of a game and will ideally go for a walk for an hour or an hour and a half. I particularly like playing in tournaments where there is some nature nearby, because I find country walks uplifting. Then after making sure I have a couple of working pens, I will get to the board five or ten minutes before the game is due to start.

The tournament at which I think I really found the right way for me personally was the Gausdal International in 1997. Before each game I went for a long walk in the Norwegian mountains, returned to the hotel for lunch and then lay down for a rest. When the time came for the game I'd just go and play, only knowing who my opponent was five minutes before I was due to commence.

Despite the fact that no chess was involved I felt superbly prepared mentally for each game and played with a very clear head and great energy. Here's a sample of my play in this tournament in which I went on to capture first place:

Game 22
N.Davies-T.Thorhallsson
Gausdal 1997
Réti Opening

---

1 ♘f3 d5 2 c4 e6 3 g3 ♘f6 4 ♗g2 ♗e7

4...dxc4 is another story.

5 0-0 0-0 6 b3

If you play this way in the opening there's no need to look at any 'theory'. The pieces will only come into conflict later on, out of the range of exact research.

6...c5 7 e3 ♘c6 8 ♕e2

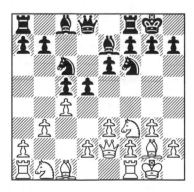

White makes no attempt to do anything direct in the centre, instead simply building up his position. For this reason the Réti is not particularly prone to theoretical investigation, depending more on understanding the concepts which unfold in the middlegame.

8...b6 9 ♗b2 ♗b7 10 ♖d1 ♖c8 11 d3 ♕c7 12 ♘c3 ♖cd8

My opponent already seemed uncomfortable and here comes up with a dubious-looking move. 12...♖fd8 was more natural.

13 ♖ac1 ♕b8 14 cxd5 ♘xd5

On 14...exd5 White plays 15 d4 followed by 16 dxc5, when Black gets either an isolated d-pawn (recapturing on c5 with a piece) or 'hanging pawns' on d5 and c5 should he recapture with the b-pawn.

15 ♘xd5 ♖xd5

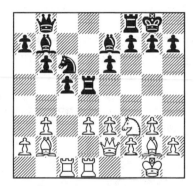

The critical reply, avoiding contracting the pawn weaknesses that would arise after 15...exd5 16 d4. Now White can try to exploit Black's temporarily misplaced rook on d5.

16 d4 cxd4 17 ♘xd4 ♘xd4 18 exd4 ♖a5!

This excellent move should keep the balance. Against 18...♖f5 I intended 19 d5 ♗c5 20 ♖xc5 bxc5 21 ♕g4 f6 (or 21...g6 22 ♗e4 ♗xd5 23 ♗xf5 exf5 24 ♕h4 etc) 22 dxe6, after which one possibility is 22...♖g5 23 ♕c4 ♔h8 24 e7 ♖e8 25 ♕b5 ♖xe7 (or 25...♗xg2 26 ♕xb8 ♖xb8 27 ♖d8+ etc) 26 ♗xb7 ♖xb7 27 ♕xb7 ♕xb7 28 ♖d8 mate.

19 d5 ♖xa2 20 dxe6 ♗xg2 21 ♔xg2 ♕b7+

The kind of error which usually decides chess games; Black has missed a finesse buried deep in a variation. He had to play 21...♗f6!, when 22 exf7+ ♔h8 23 ♖c2 ♖xb2 24 ♖xb2 ♗xb2 25 ♕xb2 ♕b7+ 26 ♔g1 ♕xf7 is equal.

22 ♔g1 ♗f6

23 ♖d7!

This could well be what Black overlooked.

23...♕a8

On 23...♖xb2 White would play 24 exf7+ ♖xf7 (or 24...♔h8 25 ♕e8 ♕a8 26 ♕xa8 ♖xa8 27 ♖e1 and 28 ♖e8) 25 ♕e8+ ♖f8 26 ♕e6+ and then take Black's queen.

24 exf7+ ♔h8

Or 24...♖xf7 25 ♕e6 ♕f8 26 ♖xf7 ♕xf7 27 ♖c8+ followed by mate.

25 ♖e1 ♖xb2 26 ♕e8!

Threatening 27 ♕xa8 followed by 28 ♖e8+. Black probably thought that his reply refuted my plan, but in the event I had seen even further.

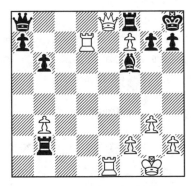

26...♖b1! 27 ♕xf8+ ♕xf8 28 ♖xb1

Interestingly, White can afford the time to do this and still bring his rook back into the attack. The threat is to play 29 ♖e1 and 30 ♖e8.

28...♗c3

One of the lines I had calculated was 28...♕c5 29 ♖e1 h5 (29...h6 allows 30 ♖e8+ ♔h7 31 f8N+ ♔g8 32 ♘e6+, winning Black's queen), when 30 ♖e8+ ♔h7 31 f8♕ ♕c1+ 32 ♔g2 ♕c6+ 33 f3 ♕xd7 34 ♕g8+ ♔h6 35 ♕e6 is simple enough. Working out such variations is a lot easier when one has a clear head, and this is the advantage of not studying chess before the game.

29 ♖bd1 g6

After 29...♗f6 White can switch to the e-file with 30 ♖e1 and then play 31 ♖e8.

30 ♖d8

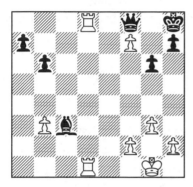

Winning the queen and thus emerging the exchange up.

30...♗b4 31 ♖xf8+ ♗xf8 32 ♖d7 a5 33 ♖b7 ♔g7 34 ♖xb6 ♔xf7 35 ♖b7+ ♔g8 1-0

With time to survey the wreckage of his position Black decided to call it a day.

Is this approach for everyone? Undoubtedly not. From a professional perspective I tend to open the game with slow and flexible openings for which it is difficult for my opponents to prepare, not to mention the fact that my repertoire is very wide. Furthermore, I used to be quite susceptible to tension during games, which preparation tended to exacerbate. So preparing via fresh air has proven to be very effective for me.

Conversely, I know that a phlegmatic player, such as Larry Christiansen, has no trouble preparing for several hours the morning before a game and cooks up many a nasty surprise. Players who adopt the sharpest lines may need even more time, but if they suffer from stress or tiredness they will definitely have a problem.

For amateurs the difficulties are even more acute: they often have to balance getting ready for a chess game with family, work and children. There is little time for any sort of preparation, especially if they have to rush to a game after a hard day's work. But despite these challenges it seems it can be done.

Just over a year ago I met one of the most interesting students with whom I've had the privilege to work, a 50-year-old Californian living in Italy called Bruce Dudley. He took my idea of rituals to new heights thanks to his expertise in relaxation and meditative techniques.

Case History: Bruce Dudley

Bruce is a self-employed chiropractor living in Italy with his wife and three children, so in addition to the usual pressures, he lives in what is essentially an alien culture. Some 16 years ago he took up chess after claiming to have found a chess computer in the jungles of Gabon in Africa. He approached me wanting to develop his game, hoping to migrate from internet chess to terrestrial tournaments in due course.

Someone in Bruce's situation is inevitably going to get distractions, and we discovered that this was the main cause of fluctuations in his playing strength. When I suggested the idea of a pre-game ritual it turned out that his knowledge of Tibetan meditative techniques could help him refocus amidst all the chaos that life could throw at him. After witnessing his success, I asked Bruce to write something for this book. Here is his own account:

"I just lost another game of chess. Exactly what I needed to motivate me to write this piece on rituals. I had been playing well this week, I was in the zone before and during each game. I like to think of it as the warrior zone. I drew and beat 2 players 125+ points above me. I felt powerful. This morning I sat down at the computer and was ready to fight with all I had. I had done my rituals and was feeling like a mind warrior. Finally my seek was answered by another player 100pts my inferior. I was ready. Then the door bell rang. The postman had a package for me that I had been waiting for. I was White about to play the Réti. So instead of aborting a game not yet begun. I mindlessly played the first moves while I did the transaction with the post person in the other room, running from one room to the

other. After about three minutes I brought my attention back to the game but I was no longer a warrior in his zone. I was just me, a little annoyed that the package was more expense than expected and not what I had wanted. I tried to rediscover the zone and focus 100% on the game. But I had lost it and played an uninspired blunder-filled game. I never really got into it.

"The account above is the main problem with playing internet chess. There are distractions. That is inevitable. I started working with Nigel about six months ago. I have gone from a struggling 1575 player with no idea how to get ahead to a strong 1775 player with potential. A great piece of advice Nigel gave me was to start a ritual. He had noticed two problems: stronger games followed by games like the one above, and more worrisome, good games where I get tripped up by the opponent's unexpected move and I self-destruct. My ritual has helped me find my zone and stay with it during the game. I am much more tenacious defender in a lost position, achieving many draws from defeat.

"Another piece of advice from Nigel was always to play seriously. Part of the problem with the blitz craze of today is that it is too easy to play haphazardly, especially when defending a difficult position. Playing carefree chess can become a habit that will influence your match games. The ritual needs to be coupled with the notion of always playing your best. We need to create routines and habits that will bring out our best play every time we sit down to play a game, so that playing our best becomes a habit. If you want to play in a more relaxed style then I would suggest to study games or teach someone how to play, which you need to distinguish in your mind from playing a game of chess.

"Routines are important in life and chess. Good daily routines for a chess player would be to study the game. Eat in a healthy manner. The brain needs high octane glucose to function its best through out the match. A glycemic spike or drop will not help your play. Breathing and meditation seem appropriate to me. To learn mindfulness and thought control can only improve your chess. Diaphragmatic breathing cannot be emphasized enough. When tense and stressed we chest breath, limiting the uptake of valuable oxygen for the brain. O_2 and glucose are what the brain need to do its work. More specific routines are how you prepare for a match. I turn on my computer. Make sure that all software is updated, especially Windows and the antivirus protection. I hate those update pop-ups when I am trying to calculate. Close the mail program and any other program that will start to bounce around during the game. Turn off the ringer on the phone. Wash my glasses. Open Dasher or Playchess and hit the seek button.

Wait. Wait. And voilà, I am playing a game of chess.

"A ritual takes the routine to the next level, to the sacred. A ritual puts us in focus so that all of our attention and energy are concentrated on the task at hand. We are entering a sacred space leaving the rest behind. All doubts, negativity, wandering thoughts are put aside until the game is finished. We need to get into the zone.

"The epitome of a pre-match ritual would be in sumo wrestling. Each move and gesture perfected and done with absolute mindfulness so that by the end of the ritual the wrestler enters the ring the ultimate warrior. The great golfers all have their individual rituals. Watch them on TV. They each have their individual way of approaching the ball. The same number of practice swings and how they position themselves to the ball for the shot done precisely the same way every time. Basketball players have the same type of rituals at the free throw line, as do tennis player at the service line. As in these sports we need to have our rituals as well. Chess, too, is a sport, but a full contact mind sport. Rituals to put our mind in order are even more important. We need to have a rehearsed ritual that we use every time before we play. It puts us in our zone. The ritual can include washing our glasses, rubbing our hands together. saying a prayer or mantra, wearing our lucky shorts, or putting a rabbit's foot in our pocket.

"I think that all of us have noticed that we play better when our minds are spacious and alert than when we are reviewing the variations of the opening we hope to play. We are more creative and flexible to the position on the board. Our task is even more daunting than in other sports. We need to maintain the zone for a longer period of time, move after move. We cannot bounce the piece off the wall three times before each move putting us back into our zone. In fact we cannot even touch the piece. This is when a physical aspect to pre-game ritual helps, that lucky pair of underpants or the rabbit's foot. We can momentarily bring our attention to the physical presence of the lucky object against our skin or in our pocket. What makes this object lucky is that it is sacred. The touching of it puts us back in the zone. All doubt and negative thoughts vanish and we are complete mind warriors ready to fight to the end. This is especially helpful when there is an unexpected move from our opponent. As we feel ourselves getting rattled then is time to feel or touch our object and get on with the game. We need to leave behind all thoughts about how the position came about and concentrate on the move at hand. We can analyze the game later.

"I explained my pre-game routine above. My pre-game ritual only changes in attitude and awareness. I turn on the computer feeling the button against my finger, a conscious act starting to find that warrior space. Updating and closing programs that could cause distractions during the game, creating a sacred space. As I check for the update and close unneeded programs, I do it with the intention of playing chess to the best of my ability and to fight to the end. I remind myself of this with each click. As I wash my glasses I try to find that relaxed alert mind that I need to play well. I let go of all thoughts of work and family. There is only the task ahead. I grab my lucky stone and open the interface to the server and click on the seek button. Now comes a hard part. I have to wait for a game. During this wait I recommit myself to the game, to playing my best come what may and fighting to the end. I also commit myself to just one or two games. No more. It is too easy to keep playing but to a substandard quality. It is better to play just one high quality game.

"I also need to decide how long I am going to wait for a game. I want to play a good quality game with enough time to think through what I am doing. Less than 20+15 is too fast for my learning process. If I can't get a game in 10 minutes my mind starts to wander. At this point I have to abandon the game and go for a tactical set or just walk away and retry later. This is a huge sacrifice for me as my time is very limited, but experience has shown that my games are sub par if I start surfing the net while I wait.

"I have another ritual during the game, endgame recognition. My endgame play has improved considerably by simply recognizing the fact that a new game has started that requires a slightly different mindset. It may only take 25 moves to reach the endgame stage and another 40+ to play it out. I think that endgame recognition has to be an essential part of the game ritual.

"The ritual by its nature is a very personal individual act. You need to play around with different ideas until you find what works for you. Then you need to stick with that ritual as it becomes a habit, a part of your game. Once you have established the ritual tinkering around with it can be very dangerous. To get some ideas try some sport psychology books, especially ones on golf and putting. Good luck finding your own way."

Bruce has experienced many ups and downs but his ability to refocus amidst life's stresses is remarkable. Let's put some meat on the bones by looking at some of his experiences:

This is the game that inspired Bruce to write the piece above and shows a vivid contrast to some of the later games in which he got "in the zone". This is not a good game as it features several serious errors, but with proper focus such errors just disappear.

> ### Game 23
> ### B.Dudley-'Dude76'
> Internet Game 2009
> *English Opening*

1 ♘f3 c5 2 c4 ♘f6 3 g3 ♘c6 4 ♗g2 e6 5 b3

5 d4 is a sharper way to play it, but Bruce likes slower build-ups from a solid position.

5...♗e7 6 ♗b2 0-0 7 0-0 ♖b8 8 ♕c2

Here, too, 8 d4 was a good move.

8...♘b4 9 ♕d1 b6 10 a3 ♘c6 11 ♘c3 ♗b7 12 d4 cxd4 13 ♘xd4 ♘xd4 14 ♕xd4 ♗xg2 15 ♔xg2 ♗c5 16 ♕f4

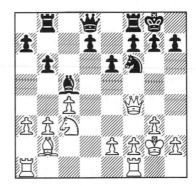

16...d5?!

Strictly speaking this is dubious, but when White chooses the wrong path Black gains equality. One of the more difficult things a player has to do is to be critical of such moves despite their happy outcome.

17 cxd5

17 ♖fd1! is a much more telling move, giving Black a major problem over his d5-pawn.

17...♘xd5 18 ♘xd5 ♕xd5+

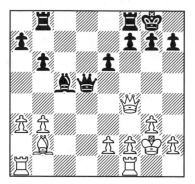

19 ♔g1

This is OK, but White has to see the possibility of a bishop sacrifice leading to perpetual check. Without this, 19 ♕f3 would have been better, covering the b3-pawn.

19...♕xb3 20 ♖ab1?

The right move was 20 ♗xg7!, when 20...♔xg7 21 ♕g5+ ♔h8 22 ♕f6+ leads to a draw by repetition. After the text White is a pawn down for nothing.

20...♕c2 21 e3 ♖bd8 22 ♖fc1 ♕g6 23 ♖d1? ♖fe8?

Both sides miss the fact that 23...♖xd1+ 24 ♖xd1 ♕c2 wins a piece.

24 ♕c7 ♖xd1+ 25 ♖xd1 a5?!

25...♕c2 was much stronger.

26 ♕d7

26 ♖d8 would make it very hard for Black to free himself; for example, after 26...f6 27 ♖d7 e5 28 a4 Black's position is completely tied up.

26...♖f8 27 a4 h6 28 ♕b5 ♕g5 29 ♗c3?

A fresh mistake which Black promptly exploits. 29 ♕d7 was better, preventing Black from bringing his rook to the d-file.

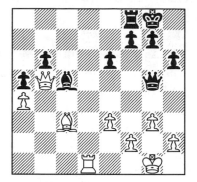

29...♗xe3! 30 ♕xg5

30 fxe3 ♕xe3+ wins the bishop on c3.

30...♗xg5 31 ♖d6 ♖c8 32 ♗d4 ♖d8 33 f4?? ♖xd6 34 fxg5 0-1

Now compare the following two games in which he was much more focused:

Game 24
'Brithem'-B.Dudley
Internet Game 2009
English Opening

"I can win again. I just needed to evoke the proper spirits. Not a great game, but I got half of my rating points back." – Bruce.

1 ♘f3 ♘f6 2 c4 c5 3 ♘c3 b6

Angling for a solid Hedgehog formation, one of Bruce's favourite set-ups with either colour. Against the English Opening it is particularly easy to achieve.

4 g3 ♗b7 5 ♗g2 e6 6 0-0 d6 7 b3 ♘bd7 8 d4 cxd4 9 ♕xd4

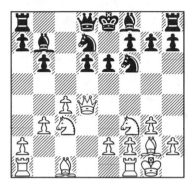

9...♘c5

A little premature; Black should settle for the prophylactic 9...a6 at this stage.

10 ♖d1 a6 11 ♗a3 ♗e7 12 ♘g5

This is a typical manoeuvre for White against the Hedgehog. The idea is to route the knight round to e4 from where it attacks the d6-pawn, though in this game the actual capture of this pawn proves problematic.

12...♗xg2 13 ♔xg2 0-0 14 ♘ge4 ♕c7 15 ♘xd6??

It looks like White may be in need of

a ritual to get focused. Internet chess seems particularly conducive to this kind of error, sleep playing into blunderdom.

15...♖ad8! 0-1

The knight on d6 is simply lost.

1 ♘f3 d5 2 c4 dxc4 3 e4!?

Bruce got this idea from my book on the Réti. The fact that he branched out from Hedgehog-style formations (which are not hard to reach after either 3 e3 or 3 ♘a3) signified a growing confidence in his tactical ability.

3...♗g4

It's probably better to play 3...c5 4 ♗xc4 ♘c6, though there's so little practical experience with 3 e4 that it's difficult to know for sure.

4 ♗xc4 e6 5 0-0 ♘f6 6 e5

This and the following moves are a

sign of alertness – White has seen the possibility of a fork on a4.

6...♘d5 7 ♗xd5!?

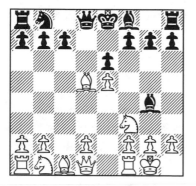

Strictly speaking, 7 ♘c3 is better, but Bruce felt in his bones that his opponent had missed the fork. And this turns out to be quite correct!

7...♕xd5??

Losing the bishop on g4. 7...exd5 was mandatory.

8 ♕a4+ ♘c6 9 ♕xg4 ♘xe5 10 ♘xe5 ♕xe5 11 d4 ♕f6 12 ♘c3

A good piece in front, the rest is essentially a mopping up operation. And White's alertness continues throughout the game, presenting no second

chances to his adversary.

12...0-0-0 13 ♗e3 h6 14 ♖ac1 ♗d6 15 ♘e4 ♕e7 16 ♘xd6+

There's no need for heroics; a lot of games are lost when the player with the better position tries to score 'extra points' for artistic impression.

16...♖xd6 17 ♕xg7 ♖dd8 18 ♗f4

Finding a new target, the pawn on c7.

18...c6 19 ♕e5 ♔d7 20 ♕c7+ ♔e8 21 ♕xe7+ ♔xe7 22 ♗e5

A tiny slip, though not too important at this stage. 22 ♗e3 would have been better, holding on to the d4 pawn.

22...f6 23 ♗g3 ♖xd4 24 ♖cd1 ♖hd8 25 ♖xd4 ♖xd4 26 f3 a6 27 ♗f2 ♖b4?

A final blunder.

28 ♗c5+ 1-0

Recently Bruce has managed to get the time to frequent a local chess club, starting the transition from internet to terrestrial chess. He has evidently found that the lessons learned about focus are just as applicable; here's his account of some recent games against a strong local player:

"Other games were ending, as was my son's lesson, and people started to gather to watch the game. I asked Tommy if he wanted to leave and he responded that he just wanted me to beat him. As the game went on, the bridge tournament finished and more people came by to watch, coming and going. What was great was that the more people who watched, the more focused I became. After a long, good game we came to the position in the second game. I knew I had a draw and saw a lot of ways to win with my move, but he didn't find the draw. So I won a good game with my first audience. My son was proud. Afterward I had no tension in my body. I had not moved for 3½ hours but felt good."

Here's the finale to the decisive game, which is a good way to round off this chapter. An ability to gain the proper focus for chess is one of the most effective abilities there is. Rituals can give you the power to do so.

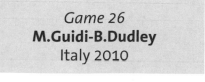

Game 26
M.Guidi-B.Dudley
Italy 2010

(see following diagram)

1...c4!

Good technique: Black is happy to sacrifice his c-pawn because he knows the pawn endgame is a win. Meanwhile the threat is 2...♖b3+.

2 ♖xc4 ♖c5!

It needs a certain amount of endgame technique to immediately realize this exchange is winning.

3 ♖xc5+ ♔xc5 4 ♔b3

After 4 h4 Black wins with 4...♔d5 5 f3 a4! 6 ♔b4 ♔d4 7 ♔xa4 ♔e3 8 f4 ♔f3 9 f5 ♔xg3 10 f6 g6!, preventing White from getting a passed pawn and then mopping up both h- and f-pawns.

4...♔d4 5 h4 ♔e4 0-1

Black will win all of White's kingside pawns.

Key Points

1. Creating a pre-game ritual can help trigger the focus and concentration required for chess and instantly improve your results.

2. A good ritual should enable you to relax and therefore concentrate. A simple routine can be just to sit in your car, listen to some pleasant music and breathe with the diaphragm.

3. Be practical about the length of the ritual depending on the typical amount of time you will have before a game. So if it's likely there will be only 10 minutes, tailor it accordingly.

4. Good sources are meditative practices such as yoga, qigong and Buddhism, as well as autogenic training and self-hypnosis. Experiment with different techniques until you find something that works for you.

Chapter Six

Cure your Time Trouble

"There are no heroes in time trouble, everyone plays badly." – Victor Korchnoi

Habitual time trouble can be a major issue for a chess player, hobbling their results severely. So many games are thrown away because of a shortage of time, ruining hours of patient work. There are countless examples of time trouble disasters, but let's look at just one:

> *Game 27*
> **C.Matamoros Franco-J.Klinger**
> World Junior Championship,
> Gausdal 1986
> *English Opening*

1 d4 d6 2 c4 e5

I quite like this defence for Black against the English. 3 dxe5 dxe5 4 ♕xd8+ ♔xd8 is harmless because Black's misplaced king is compensated for by a slight compromise (c2-c4) in White's pawn structure; and 3 ♘c3 exd4 4 ♕xd4 can lead to White losing time with his prematurely developed queen.

3 ♘f3 e4 4 ♘g5 f5 5 f3 ♘f6

5...♗e7 would be my choice, gaining time for development by attacking White's advanced knight.

6 ♘c3 ♘c6

And here, too, I would prefer 6...♗e7,

keeping the option of setting up a pawn chain in the centre with ...c7-c6 and ...d6-d5; while if 7 fxe4, Black has 7...h6 8 ♘h3 ♘xe4 9 ♘xe4 fxe4, threatening 10...♗xh3 and 11...♗h4+.

7 g3 h6 8 ♘h3 g5 9 ♘f2 exf3 10 exf3 ♗g7 11 d5 ♘e5 12 f4

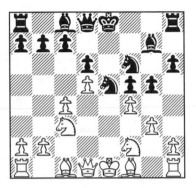

Now I like White's position because of his space advantage and Black's weakened kingside.

12...gxf4 13 ♗xf4 ♘g6 14 ♗e3 0-0 15 ♕d2 f4

Trying to drum up complications in a worsening position. At least he succeeds in getting White to think.

16 gxf4 ♗g4 17 ♗e2 ♗xe2

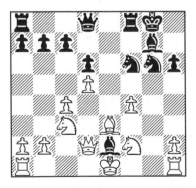

18 ♘xe2?!

18 ♕xe2 would have been better, keeping firm control over the e4-square. After 18...♘d7 19 0-0-0 ♘xf4 20 ♗xf4 ♖xf4 21 ♖hg1 White would have had strong pressure.

18...♕e7 19 ♘d4 ♘e4 20 ♘xe4 ♗xd4 21 ♕xd4 ♖ae8 22 ♖g1 ♔h7 23 f5 ♖xf5

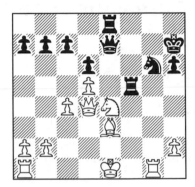

24 ♘g3?

And here White should have hurried to get his king of the e-file. Both 24 ♔d2 ♕xe4 25 ♖af1 and 24 0-0-0 ♕xe4 25 ♖g3 would have kept some pressure. In fact both players start to slip up at this point, which suggests the onset of mutual time trouble.

24...♖f4 25 ♕d2

25 ♕xa7 ♖xc4 would leave White's king in a most precarious position.

25...♕xe3+ 26 ♕xe3 ♖xe3+ 27 ♔d2 ♖e7?!

27...♖ef3 is much stronger, with threats that include 28...♖xc4 and 28...♖f2+.

28 ♖af1 ♖xc4 29 ♘h5! ♖h4 30 ♖f5 ♖xh2+ 31 ♔d1 ♖e5?

31...♖xb2 was the right move, when

32 ♘f6+ ♚g7 33 ♘h5+ would lead to a draw by perpetual check.

Now Black should lose, providing White can play the right moves before his flag falls...

32 ♖f7+ ♚g8 33 ♖g7+ ♚f8 34 ♖f1+ ♚e8 35 ♘f6+ ♚f8 0-1

Here, in terrible time trouble White touched his knight, saw that could have won with 36 ♖xg6, thought he was about to lose the rook on g7, and resigned. But with 36 ♘h5+ ♚e8 37 ♘f6+ ♚f8 (37...♚d8 38 ♖g8+ ♚e7 39 ♖e8+ ♚f7 40 ♖xe5 ♘xe5 41 ♘g4+ wins the rook), he could have simply repeated the position and then played 38 ♖xg6.

So, when horror stories like this abound, why do people allow themselves to run short of time? I believe that the main reason is simple procrastination: they cannot bring themselves to make certain decisions quickly enough at an earlier stage of the game. This itself can have several causes; for example, not understanding the posi-

tions well enough to be able to form a plan. Other reasons include an excess of perfectionism or a fear of making mistakes. Another can be that a player's approach to chess was cultivated mainly in correspondence chess: when the luxury of having vast amounts of thinking time is applied to the hurly burly of the over-the-board game, correspondence players frequently find themselves the victims of time trouble.

Let's consider each of these ideas in turn:

The issue of lacking chess understanding and planning ability can stem from studying chess in the wrong way; for example, studying the openings in a self-contained fashion without relating them properly to the middlegame. A way to iron this out is to try and learn the openings within the context of complete games, and most modern openings books take this approach.

This can be taken a stage further by studying the games with a chess set and trying out different possibilities. Most readers will do anything rather than actually analyse the material for themselves; they want the book to tell them what to do, rather than use it as a tool through which they develop their own reasoning and imagination.

It can also be of great benefit just to play through lots of games from a variety of openings so as to acquire a greater knowledge of chess patterns in general. The same ideas often crop up in totally different variations, and trying to be too specific about the kind of positions that one studies can miss this effect. Obviously it takes many thousands of hours of study and practice to acquire a Grandmaster's intuitive feel for the game, but substantial progress can be made by any player as long as he or she sets about it in the right way. During my teenage years, for example, I studied the games collections of just about every great player I could lay my hands on and was the strongest player in my town after a couple of years. This practice can be even more effective if the games are annotated by the great players themselves because you gain an insight into how they thought about chess. Once again this is a rare way of studying because it takes the kind of time that very few people are willing to spend.

Moving on to reason number two, a player can be so concerned about making a mistake that he is unable to bring himself to spread his available thinking time over the entire game. Players who do this often try to cure themselves by putting notes on the scoresheet, for example indicating how many moves they have left or how much clock time they are allowing themselves to reach a particular stage of the game.

While these efforts are well meaning I doubt they have much effect. The problem is that there is often has

deep-rooted psychological cause; for example, a time-trouble addict might have found himself criticized excessively as a child. As such it can be a very difficult problem to address, perhaps the best approach being to delve into one's inner realm through practices such as meditation. Other forms of health improvement can also help if they address someone's general anxiety levels which then carry over into the chess-playing process. I will examine this more closely in the final chapter.

A special form of perfectionism can be cultivated by correspondence chess, especially if a player relies on this exclusively. Perfectionism is actually a positive trait for correspondence games because small mistakes are likely to be exploited, but if this is then applied to over-the-board games it can result in consistent time shortage. So if you do want to make the over-the-board game your main sphere of combat, do not rely too heavily on correspondence chess for training.

The following two games are from someone who did this and serve as a good, if painful, illustration. Alexander Shalamanov came to me because he wanted to improve his over-the-board play, but his background in correspondence chess had left its mark. In both these games he showed a good general understanding, but then blundered away his queen in time trouble.

1 d4 ♘f6 2 c4 e6 3 ♘f3 d5 4 g3 ♗e7 5 ♗g2 dxc4

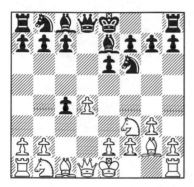

Although by no means bad, the capture at this stage feels like an indication that Black's opening repertoire is not too well worked out. Usually Black plays the more flexible 5...0-0 and only after 6 0-0 takes on c4.

6 ♕c2 a6 7 a4 0-0 8 0-0 ♘c6

8...♗d7 9 ♕xc4 ♗c6 is the solid main line and it's difficult for White to prove much here. One of the problems that Alexander had to face was that, in his correspondence games, he played very sharp openings but felt these were unsuitable over the board. So, essentially, he was left without an opening repertoire for his over-the-board games. This is why I believe the emphasis should be firmly on correspondence play for *training*; the openings played should be those one intends to use over the board.

9 ♕xc4 ♗d7

And here 9...♕d5 is a better line, though this whole variation tends to give White something of a pull.

10 ♗g5 b5 11 ♕c1 ♘a5

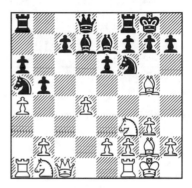

11...♖c8 12 axb5 axb5 13 ♘bd2 h6 14 ♗xf6 ♗xf6 15 ♘e4 ♕e7 (15...♗xd4 16 ♖d1 is very good for White) 16 ♖d1 ♖fd8 17 ♕c3 ♗e8 18 e3 gave White a typical, large advantage (control of c5) in A.Andres Gonzalez-J.Lobo Rodriguez, Oviedo 2006.

12 ♘bd2 h6

12...bxa4!? looks like an interesting attempt to complicate the position. Now White gets a very comfortable edge.

13 ♗xf6 ♗xf6 14 axb5 axb5 15 ♘e5 c6 16 b4

Taking control of the c5-square, which is usually an ominous sign for Black in the Catalan.

16...♗xe5 17 dxe5 ♘b7 18 ♖xa8 ♕xa8 19 ♘e4

This is one ugly position for Black.

19...♖d8

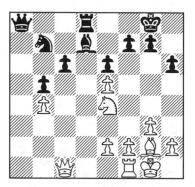

20 ♕c3

Missing an immediate win with 20 ♘f6+ gxf6 (or 20...♔f8 21 ♘xd7+ ♖xd7 22 ♕xc6) 21 exf6 ♘d6 22 ♕xh6 ♘e8 23 ♗e4 etc.

20...♗e8 21 ♖a1 ♕b8 22 f4

Further cementing White's grip.

22...♕c7 23 ♕e3 ♕e7 24 ♖a7 ♖d7 25 ♕b6 f5 26 ♘f2 ♘d8 27 ♖xd7

27 ♖a8 seems stronger.

27...♕xd7 28 ♘d3 ♘b7 29 h3 ♘d8 30 ♔h2

And here 30 ♘c5 looks more telling.

30...♗h5 31 ♘c5 ♕d2

32 ♕b8?

Suddenly White starts to mess up, suggesting time trouble all round. 32 ♕c7 was stronger, intending 32...♔h7 (or 32...♔f8 33 ♕xd8+ ♕xd8 34 ♘xe6+) 33 ♘d7 ♘f7 34 ♘f8+ ♔g8 35 ♘xe6 etc.

32...♔h7!

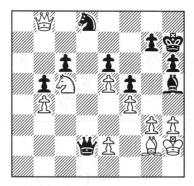

33 ♗f1?

Now the advantage changes hands! 33 ♕d6 ♕xe2 34 g4 fxg4 35 ♕xd8 gxh3 36 ♔xh3 ♕g4+ 37 ♔h2 ♕xf4+ would have led to a draw by perpetual check.

33...♗xe2 34 ♗xe2 ♕xe2+ 35 ♔g1 ♕e1+ 36 ♔g2 ♕xb4 37 ♘a6??

37 ♕d6 is a better try.

37...♕d2+ 38 ♔f3 ♕d3+ 39 ♔f2 ♕d4+ 40 ♔f3

40...♛b6??

A terrible time-trouble blunder. 40...♛c3+ 41 ♔f2 ♛b2+ 42 ♔e3 ♛a3+ is just winning for Black.

41 ♛xb6 1-0

1 e4 ♞f6

Again an opening not used by Alexander in correspondence chess; and again he struggles to find good moves early on because of his lack of familiarity with it.

2 e5 ♞d5 3 d4 d6 4 ♞f3 dxe5 5 ♞xe5 g6 6 ♗c4 ♗e6 7 ♛f3

This should not be too dangerous for Black as long as he finds the appropriate counter.

7...c6

7...♗g7 8 ♞c3 c6 is the usual response, though the move played also looks fine.

8 ♞c3 ♞d7 9 0-0 ♞xe5

9...♗g7 looks like an easier route to equality. By opening the d-file at this stage Black grants White some initiative.

10 dxe5 ♗g7 11 ♖d1

This is quite unpleasant. Black can handle it by taking on e5, but this is a scary line.

11...0-0?

Not believing he has enough time to calculate the consequences of taking on e5, Black shies away from this variation. However, it does look as if 11...♗xe5 is playable; for example, 12 ♞xd5 cxd5 13 ♗xd5 ♗xd5 14 ♖xd5 ♛c7 15 ♗h6 ♗xh2+ 16 ♔h1 ♗d6 17 ♖ad1 0-0-0 18 ♛xf7 ♔b8 with an acceptable position; certainly this is better than going a pawn down.

12 ♞xd5 ♗xd5 13 ♗xd5 cxd5 14 ♖xd5

The alternative 14 ♗f4 is also pretty good since the reply 14...e6 can be met by 15 c4.

14...♛c7 15 ♛e4 ♖ac8 16 c3 ♖fd8 17 ♗f4 ♖xd5 18 ♛xd5 ♖d8 19 ♛e4 e6

Doing the right thing by putting

pawns on light squares. Having the superior bishop will improve his drawing chances in many positions.

20 h3 ♖d5 21 ♖e1 b5 22 ♗g3 h5

This is actually the move of someone with pretty good intuition, taking the time to improve his kingside. But none of this will matter in the time-trouble phase.

23 f4 ♕d7 24 ♔h2 ♗f8 25 ♗f2

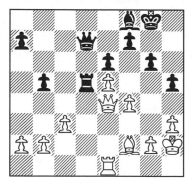

25...♗c5?!

I would not have exchanged bishops, with White's restricted by his pawns on e5 and f4. But as someone runs short of time they can find it tempting to reduce the number of

pieces, so as to have less to worry about.

26 ♗xc5 ♖xc5 27 ♖e2 ♖c4 28 ♕e3 ♕b7 29 ♖d2 b4 30 ♖d4 bxc3 31 bxc3

31 ♖xc4?! cxb2 32 ♖c1 bxc1♕ 33 ♕xc1 would probably be a draw.

31...♕c7 32 ♖xc4 ♕xc4 33 a3 a5 34 ♕d4 ♕a4?? 1-0

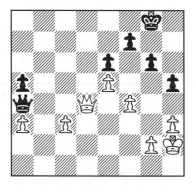

A second game with the blunder of Black's queen; this is what time trouble can do to us.

Case History: Victor Korchnoi

Very few players manage to deal successfully with curing habitual time-trouble. It requires a tremendous strength of will and self-discipline – but, as we are about to see, it can be done.

During the early part of his career Victor Korchnoi was known as a player with tremendous strengths but whose tendency to get into time trouble prevented him from getting to the top. Let's start with a couple of examples from his first match against Karpov in 1974.

1 e4 e5 2 ♘f3 ♘f6

The Petroff was one of Korchnoi's unsuccessful opening experiments in this match. By switching around he probably wanted to keep Karpov's analytical team on its toes.

3 ♘xe5 d6 4 ♘f3 ♘xe4 5 d4 d5 6 ♗d3 ♗e7 7 0-0 ♘c6

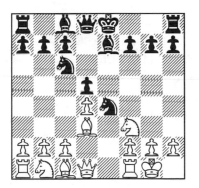

8 ♖e1

In later years 8 c4 took over as White's most testing line. A high-level example went 8...♘b4 9 ♗e2 0-0 10 ♘c3 ♗f5 11 a3 ♘xc3 12 bxc3 ♘c6 13 ♖e1 ♖e8 14 cxd5 ♕xd5 15 ♗f4 ♖ac8 16 c4 ♕e4 17 ♗e3 ♕c2!? 18 d5 ♘a5 19 ♘d4 ♕xd1 20 ♖exd1 ♗d7 and Black maintained the balance in P.Leko-V.Kramnik, World Championship (3rd matchgame), Brissago 2004.

8...♗g4 9 c3 f5 10 ♕b3 0-0 11 ♘bd2

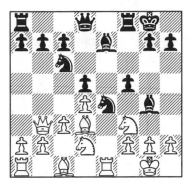

11...♔h8

In a game against Morozevich in 2002, Karpov switched to the Black side of this variation and his preference was for the rational 11...♘a5, not sacrificing a pawn. This pragmatic approach of playing good moves rather than straining for the best is worth noting for those who suffer from time trouble. After some ups and downs Karpov went on to win the game.

12 h3

Back then this was a new move, which was probably enough to start Korchnoi off on some long bouts of thinking. And before long he would be running himself short of time. Further practice revealed that 12 h3 is not really a great idea and White later gave preference to 12 ♕xb7.

12...♗h5 13 ♕xb7 ♖f6 14 ♕b3 ♖g6

The former World Champion, Mikhail Botvinnik, suggested 14...g5!?, though it isn't clear whether Black has enough compensation after 15 ♗b5, intending to take the knight on c6 and then plant his own on e5.

75

15 ♗e2

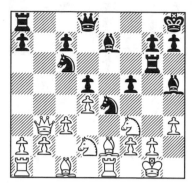

15...♗h4?

Subsequent games showed that 15...♗d6 gives Black adequate compensation for the pawn; for example, 16 ♘e5 ♘xe5 17 ♗xh5 ♖xg2+ 18 ♔xg2 ♕g5+ 19 ♔f1 ♕h4 20 ♘xe4 ♕xh3+ 21 ♔g1 fxe4 (21...♘f3+ 22 ♗xf3 ♗h2+ would also draw) 22 dxe5 ♗xe5 23 ♗e3 ♖f8 was S.Makarichev-A.Kochyev, Rostov on Don 1980, and now rather than 24 ♗f7? (which loses to 24...♗h2+ 25 ♔h1 ♗d6+ 26 ♔g1 ♖xf7), White should play 24 ♗g4! ♕xg4+ 25 ♔f1 ♖xf2+ 26 ♔xf2 (26 ♗xf2? gets mated after 26...♕h3+ 27 ♔g1 ♗h2+ 28 ♔h1 ♗g3+ 29 ♔g1 ♕h2+ 30 ♔f1 ♕xf2) 26...♕f3+ 27 ♔g1 ♕g4+ with a draw by perpetual check.

16 ♖f1 ♗xf3 17 ♘xf3 ♗xf2+?

Trying to keep it complicated but Black is simply losing after this. 17...♗e7 was better, though Black only has nebulous chances for his pawn.

18 ♖xf2 ♘xf2 19 ♔xf2 ♕d6 20 ♘g5!

Snuffing out Black's counterplay. The threat is 21 ♘f7+, winning the queen.

20...♖f8 21 ♕a3!

Trailing behind in material Black can ill afford the exchange of queens, but retreating makes his position even less promising.

21...♕d8 22 ♗f4 h6 23 ♘f3 ♖e8 24 ♗d3 ♖e4 25 g3 ♖f6 26 ♕c5 g5 27 ♘xg5

With Black running out of thinking time Karpov decides it's worth going in with the meat cleaver.

27...hxg5 28 ♗xg5 ♖ee6 29 ♖e1 ♕g8 30 h4 ♖g6 31 ♖xe6 1-0

Black lost on time in this position, but in any case the continuation 31...♖xe6 32 ♗xf5 is quite hopeless for him.

1 d4 ♘f6 2 c4 e6 3 g3 d5 4 ♗g2 dxc4 5 ♘f3 c5 6 0-0 ♘c6 7 ♕a4

These days 7 ♘e5 and 7 ♘a3 are thought to be White's most dangerous.

7...♗d7 8 ♕xc4 cxd4 9 ♘xd4 ♖c8 10 ♘c3 ♕a5 11 ♖d1 ♗e7 12 ♘b3 ♕c7

13 ♘b5

In V.Topalov-F.Pierrot, FIDE World Championship, Moscow 2001, White improved with 13 ♗f4! and went on to win a pawn 13...e5 14 ♗g5 ♗e6 15 ♕a4 0-0 16 ♗xf6 ♗xf6 17 ♘c5 ♕e7 18 ♘xe6 ♕xe6 19 ♗xc6 ♖xc6 20 ♕xa7.

13...♕b8 14 ♘c5 a6! 15 ♘xd7 ♘xd7

15...axb5 is refuted by 16 ♕xc6 bxc6 17 ♘xb8 ♖xb8 18 ♗xc6+ etc.

16 ♘c3

Not bad, but not the best. White had a stronger possibility in 16 ♘d4!, when 16...♘ce5 (or 16...♘de5 17 ♕b3)

17 ♕a4 0-0 18 ♗f4 would leave Black in serious difficulties.

It could be that Korchnoi spent time considering the exchange sacrifice 16 ♖xd7 ♔xd7 17 ♘d4, which contributed to his running short later on. This is typical of time-trouble addicts; more rational players would reject such lines quickly if they saw nothing clear.

16...♘de5

17 ♕a4

Here, too 17 ♕b3 was possible. It was probably Korchnoi's consideration of such possibilities that gradually led him into time trouble.

17...0-0 18 ♗f4 ♕a7

19 ♗xe5?!

Still looking for a large advantage. A much simpler line was 19 ♗xc6 ♘xc6 20 ♖d7 with a nagging edge for White. **19...♘xe5 20 ♕e4 ♘c6 21 ♖d7 ♗f6 22 ♖ad1 ♕b6 23 ♕c2 ♘a5 24 ♖1d3 h6 25 a3 ♖c7**

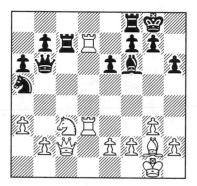

26 b4?

Korchnoi used half of his remaining ten minutes here, leaving him with just five minutes for the remaining fifteen moves. This is what costs him the game.

Had White been able to consider for longer he might have played 26 ♖3d6! first, when 26...♕c5 (26...♘c6 27 ♘a4 ♖xd7 28 ♖xd7! is also very unpleasant for Black) 27 b4 ♕c4 (27...♕xc3 28 ♖xc7 wins the exchange) 28 bxa5 ♗xc3 29 ♗xb7 leaves White with all the chances.

26...♖xd7

Not 26...♘c4 because of 27 ♘a4!.

27 ♖xd7 ♖c8 28 ♖d3

After 28 bxa5 ♕xa5 Black would simply win back the knight.

There was, however, a strong line in

28 ♘d5!, after which 28...♖xc2 29 ♘xb6 ♖c1+ 30 ♗f1 ♘b3 31 e3 followed by 32 ♔g2 is still very good for White.
28...♘c4 29 ♘e4 ♕c7! 30 ♘c5?

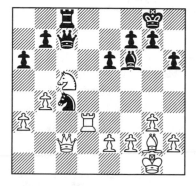

30 ♘xf6+ gxf6 31 ♗f1 would still have been OK; after the text White is worse.

30...♘e5!

Botvinnik thought that 30...♘b2?! was good, but White can answer this by 31 ♖d2! b6 32 ♗b7 bxc5 33 ♗xc8 ♕xc8 34 bxc5 with a big passed c-pawn and the black knight trapped.

31 ♖d2?

31 ♖c3 would have made it harder for Black, but he's still winning after 31...b6 32 ♗b7 (or 32 ♘e4 ♘f3+ 33 ♗xf3 ♗xc3 etc) 32...♖d8! 33 ♘xe6! ♘f3+ 34 ♗xf3 ♕xc3 35 ♕xc3 ♖d1+! 36 ♔g2 ♗xc3 37 ♘c7 ♖a1 38 ♘xa6 ♖xa3 39 b5 ♗e5! 40 ♘b4 ♖b3 41 ♘d3 ♖xb5, as pointed out by Botvinnik.

31...b6 32 f4 bxc5 33 fxe5 ♕xe5

Black has emerged a good pawn up, with White's king position being weakened into the bargain.

34 ♗b7

34 ♔f2 was relatively best here.
34...♖c7 35 ♕e4 ♕a1+ 36 ♔g2 ♕xa3 37 bxc5 ♖xc5 38 ♖d3 ♕a5 39 ♕f3 ♕b6 40 ♖d7?

A blunder, which curtails White's resistance.
40...♖f5 41 ♕g4 ♕f2+ 42 ♔h3 g6! 0-1

With Karpov being much younger than him and an ideal representative of the Soviet Union, it looked like this match was Korchnoi's last chance in the World Championship. But then something remarkable happened, starting with his defection in 1976.

Free from the shackles of the Soviet state, Korchnoi set about achieving his goal. To this end he successfully managed to change his style from being a time-troubled grabber of material, to becoming much more of an all-rounder and staying out of time trouble whenever possible. The reborn Victor Korchnoi achieved match triumphs over rivals, such as Lev Polugaevsky and the former World Champion Boris Spassky, to earn a title match against Karpov. And he came within a whisker of winning that one too.

Here, first of all, are two of his games from the Candidates matches which show the transformation in his play. Rather than being his enemy the clock was starting to become his friend and he began exploiting his opponents' time trouble.

> ### Game 32
> ### L.Polugaevsky-V.Korchnoi
> ### Candidates semi-final,
> ### (6th matchgame) Evian 1977
> ### *English Defence*

1 d4 e6 2 c4 b6!? 3 e4

According to Raymond Keene, one of Korchnoi's seconds during the match, Polugaevsky played this move with an 'air of disbelief'. The shock value of 2...b6 was already working.
3...♗b7 4 ♕c2

Intending to defend the e4-pawn without allowing the doubled c-pawns that would arise after 4 ♘c3 ♗b4 5

♕c2 (5 ♗d3 f5!) 5...♕h4 6 ♗d3 ♗xc3+ 7 bxc3. But after Black's reply Polugaevsky sank into thought for a full nineteen minutes.

4...♕h4! 5 ♘d2 ♗b4 6 ♗d3 f5 7 ♘gf3 ♗xd2+ 8 ♔f1?

Disorientated by the unexpected start to the game, White produces a poor move which maintains material equality only at the cost of a bad position.

He should have played 8 ♗xd2 ♕g4 9 ♘e5 ♕xg2 10 0-0-0, as in I.Rogers-R.Lau, Wijk aan Zee 1989, when 10...fxe4 11 ♗e2 ♘f6 12 ♗e3 ♕h3! 13 ♖dg1 ♘c6! (rather than 13...h6? 14 ♖xg7 ♘c6 15 ♘g6! and White was clearly better) 14 ♖g3 (now 14 ♖xg7?! ♘xd4! 15 ♗xd4 ♕h6+ 16 ♔b1 ♕xg7 17 ♘g4 ♖f8 18 ♕c3 ♔e7 is good for Black) 14...♕f5 15 ♘xc6 (and not 15 ♖g5? ♘xd4!) 15...♗xc6 16 ♖g5 ♕h3 17 ♖g3 ♕f5 is one possible draw by repetition.

8...♕h5 9 ♗xd2 ♘f6 10 exf5 ♗xf3 11 gxf3 ♘c6!

Emphasizing speedy development.

12 ♗c3 0-0 13 ♖e1 ♕h3+

Evidence of a very different Victor Korchnoi to the one who liked to take pawns. Here he rejects 13...♕xf3 in favour of pursuing the initiative.

14 ♔e2 ♖ae8 15 ♔d1 e5!

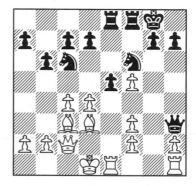

Once again spurning pawns to keep the initiative. The position bears some resemblance to a reverse King's Gambit, about which Korchnoi once co-authored a book together with Vladimir Zak.

16 dxe5 ♘xe5 17 ♗e2

After 17 ♗xe5 ♖xe5 18 ♖xe5 ♕xf3+ Black picks up the rook on h1.

17...♘xf3! 18 ♕d3 ♖xe2! 19 ♖xe2

19 ♔xe2 is met by 19...♕h5!, when 20 ♕xf3 ♖e8+ wins White's queen.

19...♕g2

The point behind Black's play: he wins back the exchange with a clear advantage thanks to White's ragged position.

20 ♖he1 ♘xe1 21 ♔xe1 ♕xh2?

Inaccurate. 21...♕g1+ 22 ♔d2 ♕xh2 was better, since 23 ♖e7? could then be met by 23...♕xf2+.

22 ♖e7! ♕g1+ 23 ♔e2 ♕g4+ 24 ♔e1 h5

25 ♕g3!

A superb defensive move by Polugaevsky. The exchange of queens is the best way to safeguard his king, and the endgame offers excellent drawing chances.

25...♕xg3 26 fxg3 ♖f7 27 ♗xf6! gxf6 28 ♖e8+ ♔g7 29 ♔f2

Although Black is a pawn up the position is extremely difficult to win because of the dominating position of White's rook.

29...♔h6 30 b4 ♔g5 31 ♖a8 ♔xf5 32 ♖xa7 d6 33 a4 ♔e6 34 a5 bxa5 35 ♖xa5 f5 36 c5 ♖h7 37 cxd6 cxd6 38 b5 h4 39 gxh4 ♖xh4 40 ♖a8 ♖b4 41 ♖b8 ♔d5

42 ♔f3?!

Polugaevsky's sealed move, on which he thought for 51 minutes, leaving himself with just 8 minutes for the remaining 14 moves. It should still draw, but it's not the best: the simplest way was 42 ♖b6!, when 42...♔c5 43 ♖c6+ stops Black making any progress.

42...♖b3+!?

Having seen that the main lines led to a draw, and assuming Polugaevsky and his team would have them well worked out, Korchnoi chooses an apparently useless check in order to make his opponent think. And it works...

43 ♔f4 ♔c5 44 ♖c8+?

Under pressure from the clock Polugaevsky makes a losing blunder. He should have played 44 ♔xf5 immediately, when it would be a draw.

44...♔xb5 45 ♔xf5 ♖e3

Cutting White's king off.

46 ♔f4 ♖e1 47 ♖d8 ♔c5 48 ♖c8+ ♔d4 49 ♔f3 d5 50 ♔f2 ♖e5 51 ♖a8 ♔c3 52 ♖a3+ ♔b4 53 ♖a1 d4 54 ♖c1 d3 55 ♖c8 d2 56 ♖b8+ ♔c3 57 ♖c8+ ♔d3 58 ♖d8+ ♔c2 59 ♖c8+ ♔d1 0-1

Black wins by the famous Lucena method; i.e. 60 ♖c7 ♖f5+ 61 ♔g2 (61 ♔e3 ♔e1 will promote next move) 61...♔e2 62 ♖e7+ ♔d3 63 ♖d7+ ♔e3 64 ♖e7+ (or 64 ♖d8 ♖f4 threatening 65...♖d4) 64...♔d4 65 ♖d7+ ♖d5 and wins.

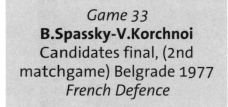

Game 33
B.Spassky-V.Korchnoi
Candidates final, (2nd matchgame) Belgrade 1977
French Defence

1 e4 e6 2 d4 d5 3 ♘c3 ♗b4 4 e5 c5 5 a3 ♗xc3+ 6 bxc3 ♘e7 7 ♕g4

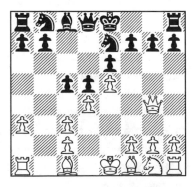

Although Bobby Fischer claimed that the Winawer Variation (3...♗b4) was "anti-positional and weakened the kingside", he never played this critical move.

7...cxd4

Recently there has been a greater focus on 7...0-0.

8 ♕xg7 ♖g8 9 ♕xh7 ♕c7 10 ♘e2

10 ♔d1!? used to be White's other main move.

10...♘bc6 11 f4 ♗d7 12 ♕d3 dxc3 13 ♗e3 d4!?

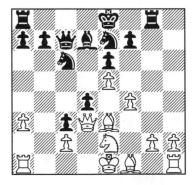

Korchnoi had deliberately prepared this line to put Spassky in the uncomfortable role of having to defend. Black must sacrifice a pawn or two, but he gets the initiative.

14 ♗f2 0-0-0 15 ♘xd4 ♘xd4 16 ♕xd4 b6 17 ♗h4 ♗b5 18 ♕e4 ♗xf1 19 ♖xf1

Playing to win? White had a forced draw here with 19 ♕a8+ ♔d7! (19...♕b8 20 ♕xb8+ ♔xb8 21 ♔xf1 is good for White) 20 0-0-0+ ♘d5 21 ♖xd5+ exd5 22 ♕xd5+ ♔c8 23 ♕a8+ etc.

19...♖d5! 20 ♗xe7 ♕xe7 21 ♖f3 ♔b8

22 ♔f1?!

After this Black is better. White should have played 22 g3!, when 22...♕c5 23 ♕e3 ♖d4 24 ♔f1 is about equal.

22...♖d2 23 ♖f2 ♖gd8 24 ♕f3 ♖xf2+ 25 ♔xf2 ♖d2+ 26 ♔g3

26 ♔f1 ♕c5 would have left White completely tied up while regaining the pawn; for example, 27 ♖c1 ♕b5+ 28 ♔g1 (or 28 ♔e1 ♕b2) 28...♖xc2 is good.

26...♕d8!

Not 26...♖xc2?, as 27 ♖d1 would give White some counterplay.

27 ♕e4 ♕g8+ 28 ♔h3 ♕h8+ 29 ♔g3 ♕g7+ 30 ♔h3 ♖d8

Threatening mate with 31...♖h8+.

31 g4

31 g3 ♕h6+ 32 ♔g2 ♖d2+ is a mating attack.

31...♖h8+ 32 ♔g3 ♕h6 33 ♕g2 ♕h4+ 34 ♔f3 ♖d8 35 ♕g3

35 ♖f1 would have been better, so as to meet 35...♖d2 with 36 ♖f2.

35...♕e7 36 g5?

In time trouble Spassky misses his last chance. 36 ♖e1 was the best try.

36...♖d2 37 ♔g4 ♕b7 38 ♕xc3 ♖g2+ 39 ♔h3 ♖f2 40 ♔g4 ♕e4 0-1

Finally, here's the game which took Korchnoi to a 5-5 win tally in his Baguio City match against Karpov and within a whisker of the Championship title.

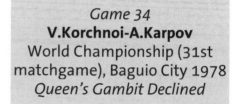

Game 34
V.Korchnoi-A.Karpov
World Championship (31st matchgame), Baguio City 1978
Queen's Gambit Declined

1 c4

The English Opening is a good way of avoiding the Nimzo-Indian Defence, a firm favourite of Karpov.

1...e6 2 ♘c3 d5 3 d4 ♘f6 4 cxd5 exd5 5 ♗g5 ♗e7 6 e3 0-0 7 ♗d3 ♘bd7 8 ♘f3

Another promising line for White is 8 ♘ge2, the so-called Carlsbad Variation. White then has the possibility of advancing in the centre with a later f2-f3 and e3-e4, as well as on the queenside.

8...♖e8 9 ♕c2 c6 10 0-0 ♘f8 11 ♗xf6

One of many moves for White in this position.

11...♗xf6 12 b4 ♗g4 13 ♘d2 ♖c8 14 ♗f5

Exchanging off one of Black's bishops.

14...♗xf5 15 ♕xf5

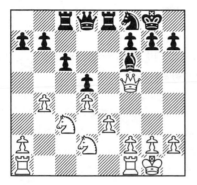

15...♕d7

15...g6?! 16 ♕d3 ♕d6 17 ♖fb1 ♗g7 18 a4 was good for White in S.Reshevsky-L.Myagmarsuren, Sousse Interzonal 1967, with a minority attack on the queenside (White's idea is to play an eventual b4-b5), while Black had little counterplay on the other flank.

I don't see that the exchange of queens makes much sense either, because White will still have his minority attack, and it will be very difficult for Black to generate counter-chances. I think Karpov was probably influenced by the match situation and his great desire to make a draw with Black.

16 ♕xd7 ♘xd7 17 a4 ♗e7 18 ♖fb1 ♘f6 19 a5!?

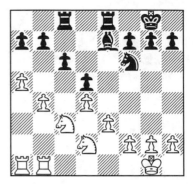

A very interesting decision: rather than proceed with a standard minority attack (b4-b5), Korchnoi wants to target Black's b7-pawn by bringing a knight to c5. The drawback is that he will need to break through elsewhere, so his plan is to expand in the centre with f2-f3 and e3-e4.

19...a6 20 ♘a4 ♗f8

20...♗d6 21 ♘c5 ♖e7 and ...♖ce8 might have been better, so as to inhibit White's plan of e3-e4.

21 ♘c5 ♖e7 22 ♔f1 ♘e8 23 ♔e2 ♘d6 24 ♔d3 ♖ce8

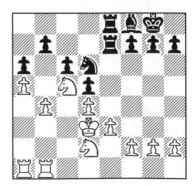

25 ♖e1

Commencing the next stage of his

strategy.

25...g6 26 ♖e2 f6

A bit passive; Black should have tried to prevent e3-e4 with ...f7-f5. White would play f2-f4 and then bring his d2-knight to e5 via f3, but this would be a better chance for Black than waiting for the enemy to reach his gates.

27 ♖ae1 ♗h6 28 ♘db3 ♗f8 29 ♘d2 ♗h6 30 h3 ♔f7 31 g4 ♗f8 32 f3 ♖d8

33 ♘db3

33 e4 was already a possibility, but Korchnoi wanted to reach the time control first, so he could work out how to break through at more leisure. This controlled approach to clock handling was not previously present in Korchnoi's play.

33...♘b5 34 ♖f1 ♗h6 35 f4 ♗f8 36 ♘d2 ♘d6 37 ♖fe1 h6 38 ♖f1 ♖b8 39 ♖a1 ♖be8 40 ♖ae1 ♖b8 41 e4

Finally playing his trump card.

41...dxe4+ 42 ♘dxe4 ♘b5 43 ♘c3

Karpov's last move set a trap. At first 43 f5 looks very strong, but after 43...gxf5 44 gxf5 ♖d8 45 ♘e6 ♖ed7! 46

♘xd8+ ♖xd8 the d4-pawn falls and Black gains excellent counterplay for the exchange.

43...♖xe2 44 ♖xe2 ♗xc5 45 bxc5 ♖d8 46 ♘xb5 axb5 47 f5 gxf5

Karpov sealed this move so he could analyse the position with his seconds during the adjournment. Objectively speaking it should be a draw, but this endgame is highly complex.

48 gxf5 ♖g8

After 48...♖a8 White would play 49 ♖a2 and then bring his king to b4 before breaking through with d4-d5.

49 ♔c3!?

49 ♖a2 was the obvious move, which made it more likely to have been studied by Karpov's team.

49...♖e8

49...♖g3+? 50 ♔b4 ♖xh3 is bad because of 51 a6! bxa6 52 d5! ♖h4+ (or 52...cxd5 53 c6 ♖h4+ 54 ♔c5 ♖c4+ 55 ♔xd5) 53 ♔a5 cxd5 54 ♖c2, when suddenly White's c-pawn is a monster.

50 ♖d2 ♖e4 51 ♔b4 ♔e8 52 a6

Getting the king through at the cost of a pawn. White's idea is to create a passed c-pawn with d4-d5 but wants his king on b6 first.

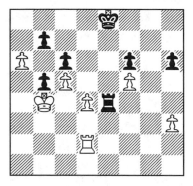

52...bxa6 53 ♔a5 ♔d7 54 ♔b6 b4 55 d5 cxd5 56 ♖xd5+ ♔c8 57 ♖d3 a5?

Starting to lose his way. 57...♖c4! was the correct move, after which 58 ♖g3 ♖c3 59 ♖g2 b3 60 c6 ♖d3 61 ♖g8+ ♖d8 62 ♖g7 b2 63 ♖c7+ ♔b8 64 ♖b7+ is a draw.

58 ♖g3 b3 59 ♔c6! ♔b8?

After this Black is clearly losing. 59...♖d4 was a better try, when 60 ♖xb3 a4 61 ♖b5 h5 gives him some drawing chances.

60 ♖xb3+ ♔a7 61 ♖b7+ ♔a6 62 ♖b6+ ♔a7 63 ♔b5

Now Black's pawns are falling like ripe apples.

63...a4 64 ♖xf6 ♖f4 65 ♖xh6 a3 66 ♖a6+ ♔b8 67 ♖xa3 ♖xf5 68 ♖g3

The smoke has finally cleared to reveal a winning endgame for White.

68...♖f6 69 ♖g8+ ♔c7 70 ♖g7+ ♔c8 71 ♖h7 1-0

I have wondered whether there was a magic ingredient to Korchnoi's cure for his time trouble addiction, and I think I discovered a clue when we looked over our game from the 2009 Staunton Memorial Tournament. Korchnoi kept saying there was "nothing to calculate" whenever there was a line without forcing variations, and it seemed like a very deliberate mantra. I believe this is what he had learned which led to the improvement in his game, that there are times to crunch variations and others when one must play by feel.

Key Points

1. Try to identify the cause of your time trouble. Usually it is the attempt to calculate incalculable positions, but the reasons why someone would try to do so can be quite varied, from perfectionism to procrastination to poor positional understanding.

2. Have it clear in your mind that improper use of your thinking time is hobbling your results and resolve to play more of your moves intuitively. The more you do this the better you will get at it.

3. If you do find yourself in time trouble, try to avoid going for critical variations. Instead, it is better just to keep the position fairly stable with some consolidating moves.

Chapter Seven

Read a Good Book

One of the great things about chess, as opposed to disciplines such as ballroom dancing, is that you can learn a lot from the right books. Accordingly I count myself very fortunate in having many of the greatest players in history as my teachers.

Special mention should go to Emanuel Lasker, Mikhail Botvinnik, Paul Keres, Alexander Kotov and Bent Larsen. I also learned a lot from books by Hans Kmoch, Raymond Keene, Leonard Barden and Steffen Zeuthen – the latter two being lesser lights, but that does not stop them from offering important insights providing someone reads their books in the right way.

Judging from the reviews of various chess books that I have seen, this is not the way that most people do it. Instead of using them as a tool for the development of their own thinking, people want the book to tell them the 'secret' of good chess. When they go in with this attitude it is hardly surprising that disappointment awaits. In my view a chess book should be there to inspire rather than instruct, because the best lessons are those which we learn via our own experience. For me a chess book proves worthwhile if it simply starts me thinking about something in a new way.

I have read hundreds of chess books and found every one of them helpful to some degree. The following are particularly memorable to me personally, often for what seem like quite unusual reasons. But they all contributed towards my development as a player.

The Right Way to Play Chess
(Imre König)

I still have a battered old copy of this book which was one of my very first. Although it is billed as a book for beginners I tend to believe it advances rather too quickly for most newcomers to the game. What I found useful were the game annotations and the section on how to make your castled king secure, comparing different types of castled positions. This provided an early introduction to the importance of patterns and king safety.

The Guardian Chess Book (Leonard Barden)

It may seem like a surprising choice but in fact this was one of the most useful chess books I had during my teenage years. It is essentially an introduction to chess in which Barden explains the rules, gives some general advice and some puzzles. But the best part for me was the section on "method chess", where Barden presented certain opening systems such as the Scotch Gambit, the Chigorin Defence and the King's Indian Attack.

These formed the basis of my early opening repertoire and I still play the King's Indian Attack to this day. Here's a game of mine with this opening that helped me to third place in the 2008 British Championship.

Game 35
N.Davies-D.Kolbus
British Championship,
Liverpool 2008
Réti Opening

1 g3

One of my favourite opening moves these days, putting the emphasis firmly on positional understanding.

1...d5 2 ♘f3 ♘f6 3 ♗g2 c6 4 0-0 g6 5 d3 ♗g7 6 ♘bd2 0-0 7 e4

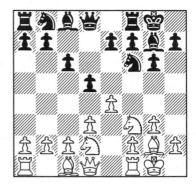

7...dxe4

One of the problems with this exchange is that, with Black's d5-pawn off the board, White gets access to the e4-square. On the other hand, if Black does not play ...d5xe4 he has to consider the possibility that White may capture on d5 himself. For example, R.Dzindzichashvili-T.Giorgadze, Tbilisi 1970, went 7...♘bd7 8 ♖e1 e5 9 exd5 ♘xd5 10 ♘c4 ♕c7 11 a4 b6 12 h4 ♗a6 13 h5 ♖fe8 14 hxg6 hxg6 15 ♘g5 ♘f8 16 a5 ♘e6 17 ♘xe6 ♖xe6 18 axb6 axb6 19 ♗g5, when Black's position was rather loose, especially on the kingside.

8 dxe4 ♕c7

Black has chosen a conservative set-up, but it is one in which White has a pleasant space advantage. This is especially the case when my e-pawn advances to e5. In the game R.J.Fischer-A.Feuerstein, New York (blitz) 1971,

Black played 8...♘bd7 9 ♖e1 e5 to prevent this, but after 10 ♘c4 ♕e7 11 b3 b5 12 ♗a3 b4 13 ♗b2 White had a clear advantage since 13...♘e8 would be met by 14 a3.

9 ♕e2 ♘fd7 10 ♖e1 ♘a6

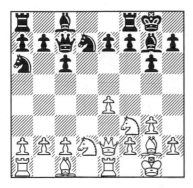

Black could stop White's next move by again playing 10...e5 himself, but this would weaken the d6-square.

11 e5 ♘dc5 12 ♘b3 ♘e6 13 ♗d2 ♘ac5 14 ♕c4

14...♘xb3

After this I was very happy with my position because the half-open a-file will give Black trouble for a long time to come. Instead, 14...b6 was worth

considering, though White can then limber up for a kingside attack with 15 ♘xc5 ♘xc5 16 ♕h4.

15 axb3 ♖d8 16 h4

Probing the kingside like this is something I learned from *The Guardian Chess Book*. Black decides to take the bull by the horns to pre-empt White's attack, but it does look like an overreaction.

16...♖xd2?!

After 16...b5 I would have played 17 ♕e4 followed by 18 h5, but this is probably preferable for Black to just giving up material. The game now enters a technical phase in which I finally manage to bring home the bacon.

17 ♘xd2 ♗xe5 18 c3 a6 19 ♘f3 ♗f6 20 ♖ad1 h5 21 b4 ♗d7 22 ♔h2

There's no need to hurry; it's better to improve the position gradually.

22...♖f8 23 ♗h3 ♗c8 24 ♔g2 ♘g7 25 ♗xc8 ♕xc8 26 ♘e5

The threats of 27 ♘xg6 and 27 ♘d7 force further simplification.

26...♗xe5 27 ♖xe5 ♕c7 28 ♖e2 ♖d8?!

This allows me to get the queens

off. 28...♘f5 would have been more tenacious.

29 ♕f4! ♖c8 30 ♕xc7 ♖xc7 31 ♖d8+ ♔h7 32 ♖ed2 c5

33 bxc5?!

33 ♖2d7 was a lot simpler. With the win in sight I was getting a bit complacent.

33...♖xc5 34 ♖8d7 ♘f5 35 ♖xb7 ♔g7 36 ♖b6 a5 37 b4

Passed pawns should be pushed.

37...axb4 38 cxb4 ♖c7 39 b5 ♘d6 40 ♖b8 ♔f6 41 b6 ♖d7 42 ♖b2 ♔e6 43 ♔f3 ♘c4 44 ♖c2 ♖d4 45 ♔e2 ♘d6 46 ♖b2 ♖e4+ 47 ♔d3 ♖a4 48 ♖c8!

48...♔d7

After 48...♘xc8 49 b7 the pawn queens.

49 ♖c7+ 1-0

Lasker's Manual of Chess (Emanuel Lasker)

This is my all-time favourite chess book written by one of the greatest players and thinkers in the history of the game. Although the book is supposedly for beginners, players of every level can benefit from reading it. Lasker's wisdom and philosophical insights shine through on every page, making it a genuine treasure of chess literature.

I have read it from cover to cover about four times and dipped into it on many other occasions. Every time I do so I learn something new, with Lasker's lessons being applicable to fields beyond the chessboard.

The following game is my favourite by Lasker, his win against Capablanca at the great St. Petersburg tournament of 1914. It is highly instructive in many different ways; for example, on a technical level the move f4-f5 is very interesting. As far as chess psychology is concerned it is a masterpiece.

> ## Game 36
> ### Em.Lasker-J.R.Capablanca
> St Petersburg 1914
> *Ruy Lopez*

1 e4 e5 2 ♘f3 ♘c6 3 ♗b5 a6 4 ♗xc6

Given the tournament situation, in which Lasker had to win in order to fight for first place, the choice of this line was a psychological masterstroke. The Exchange Lopez has the reputation of being drawish, but Black must play actively in order to utilize his two bishops. Should he play passively, on the other hand, White's superior pawn structure becomes the most important factor.

4...dxc6 5 d4

Half a century later Bobby Fischer would resurrect the Exchange Variation with 5 0-0. This had previously been thought risky because of 5...♗g4 6 h3 h5, but Fischer decided this was good for White; for example, 7 d3 ♕f6 8 ♘bd2 ♘e7 (after 8...g5 White has 9 ♘c4! ♗xf3 10 ♕xf3 ♕xf3 11 gxf3 f6 12 h4! gxh4 13 f4 with more than enough for the pawn) 9 ♖e1 ♘g6 10 d4 ♗d6 11 hxg4 hxg4 12 ♘h2 ♖xh2 13 ♕xg4 ♖h4 14 ♕f5 sees White beat off the attack with the better game.

5...exd4 6 ♕xd4 ♕xd4 7 ♘xd4 ♗d6 8 ♘c3 ♘e7 9 0-0!?

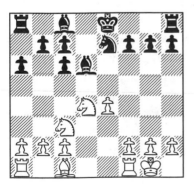

This was unusual at the time, preference being given to castling long. The logic behind castling short is that White's king is better placed to support the advance of the kingside pawns, while the downside is that it may be less secure. But Lasker is banking on his opponent playing for a draw and simplifying whenever possible, in which case having an active king is to White's advantage.

9...0-0 10 f4

10...♖e8

Developing the rook to a logical square, but already this move is a little passive. Black should have played the forthright 10...f5!, after which 11 e5 ♗c5 12 ♗e3 ♗xd4! 13 ♗xd4 b6 14 ♖ad1 c5 15 ♗e3 ♗e6 leaves White with a passed pawn, but one which is firmly blockaded by the bishop on e6. Chances would be about equal here because the e6-bishop even derives strength from its position.

The immediate 10...♗c5 would be less good because of 11 ♗e3 ♖d8 12 ♖ad1 ♗g4 13 ♖d3 ♖d7 14 h3 ♖ad8 15 hxg4 ♗xd4 16 ♗xd4 ♖xd4 17 ♖xd4 ♖xd4 18 ♖d1, when the position has simplified and White's pawn majority is the healthier (in that it is more likely to yield a passed pawn). Even so this position would not be easy to win.

11 ♘b3 f6

Again rather passive. 11...♗e6 was a better move, when 12 e5 is well met by 12...♗b4.

12 f5!?

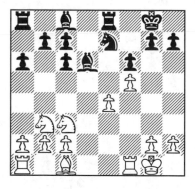

Another surprising move from Lasker, as surrendering the e5-square appears to cripple his kingside. But he has rightly seen that the pawns need to harmonize with his remaining dark-squared bishop, so he therefore puts them on light squares. Meanwhile the f5-pawn makes it difficult for Black to get his pieces working, particularly the bishop on c8 and knight on e7.

12...b6

12...♗d7 would have been better, after which 13 ♗f4 can be met by 13...♗xf4 14 ♖xf4 ♖ad8.

13 ♗f4 ♗b7?!

Played after a long thought and again not the best. Black should have tried 13...♗xf4 14 ♖xf4 c5, keeping the b3-knight at bay for a while. Even so the position looks quite good for White after 15 ♖d1 ♗b7 16 ♖f2 ♖ad8 17 ♖xd8 ♖xd8 18 ♖d2 ♖xd2 19 ♘xd2 because his kingside pawn majority will be able to yield a passed pawn.

14 ♗xd6

Undoubling Black's pawns but leaving him with a new weakness on d6.

14...cxd6 15 ♘d4

Now White's knight heads to the powerful d6-square. Black's position is already quite difficult.

15...♖ad8?!

15...♖a7 was preferable, so as to meet 16 ♖ad1 with 16...♗c8. Even so White would have much the better of it after 17 g4, followed by a retreat of his knight from d4 and then targeting the d6-pawn.

16 ♘e6 ♖d7 17 ♖ad1 ♘c8

The bid for counterplay with 17...d5 can be answered by 18 ♘a4 ♘c8 19 exd5 cxd5 20 g4 with a dominating position for White.

18 ♖f2 b5 19 ♖fd2 ♖de7

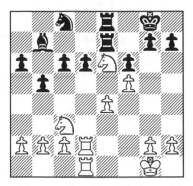

20 b4!

Ruling out both ...c6-c5 and ...b5-b4.

20...♔f7 21 a3 ♗a8 22 ♔f2

Calmly strengthening his position and preparing to advance the kingside pawns.

22...♖a7 23 g4 h6 24 ♖d3 a5

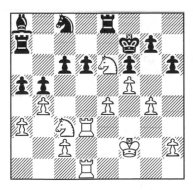

Trying to obtain some counterplay, but the opening of the a-file ultimately helps White.

25 h4 axb4 26 axb4 ♖ae7?!

Promptly abandoning the newly opened file.

27 ♔f3 ♖g8 28 ♔f4 g6 29 ♖g3 g5+ 30 ♔f3 ♘b6

Or 30...gxh4 31 ♖h3, recovering the h4-pawn and then targeting h6.

31 hxg5

Black was probably hoping for 31 ♖xd6?! ♘c4 followed by 32...♘e5+ with counterplay. Of course Lasker is having none of it.

31...hxg5 32 ♖h3 ♖d7

33 ♔g3!

Getting ready for the decisive breakthrough with e4-e5.

33...♔e8 34 ♖dh1

Further preparation for e4-e5 by removing his rook from the d-file. Lasker is in no hurry.

34...♗b7 35 e5!

Finally – and freeing e4 for White's c3-knight is completely decisive.

35...dxe5

The alternatives are no better; e.g.:

a) 35...d5 36 exf6 ♔f7 37 ♘c5 wins at least the exchange.

b) 35...fxe5 36 ♘e4 ♘d5 37 ♖h8 ♖xh8 38 ♖xh8+ ♔e7 39 ♘6xg5 ♘f6 40 ♘xf6 ♔xf6 41 ♖h6+ ♔e7 (41...♔xg5 42 ♖g6 is an immediate mate) 42 f6+ ♔d8 43 ♖h8+ ♔c7 44 f7 and Black must part with his rook.

36 ♘e4 ♘d5 37 ♘6c5 ♗c8

White is winning the exchange, as after 37...♖e7 there is 38 ♘xb7 ♖xb7 39 ♘d6+ etc.

38 ♘xd7 ♗xd7 39 ♖h7 ♖f8 40 ♖a1 ♔d8 41 ♖a8+ ♗c8 42 ♘c5 1-0

Black cannot meet the threats of 43 ♖d7+, 43 ♘b7+ and 43 ♘e6+.

Think like a Grandmaster (Alexander Kotov)

This is one of the all-time classic chess books and one which has been avidly studied by generations of chess players. At the time of publication it was light years ahead of any other book on the market, because of the sophistication of the ideas about what makes a strong player.

Inspired by the section on analysis I made a regular practice of setting up complex positions and then writing down my analysis. There were many other things I got from it, too, but this was the most valuable.

Sahovski Olympiad Havana 1966 (Sahovski Informator)

This was my first tournament book: a Yugoslav collection of games from the Havana Olympiad, categorized by opening but without any notes. It took me some time to figure out the symbol for each of the pieces, but once I had done this I took to Serbo-Croat algebraic notation like a duck to water. Over the next few years I wrote my moves down using this form of notation, which probably annoyed the hell out of many of the adults I played in the local league.

The Middle Years of Paul Keres (by Paul Keres)

My father brought this one home for me one day and it would have a profound influence on my game. Keres has been one of my favourite players ever since and one of the major influences on the way that I play. For example, I defended against the Ruy Lopez with a Keres favourite, the Steinitz Deferred (1 e4 e5 2 ♘f3 ♘c6 3 ♗b5 a6 4 ♗a4 d6) and later switched to another one of his lines, 4...♘f6 5 0-0 ♗e7 6 ♖e1 b5 7 ♗b3 d6 8 c3 0-0 9 h3 ♘a5 10 ♗c2 c5 11 d4 ♘d7!?.

One of the games from the book that made a big impression on me was the following win against Taimanov. As a result of seeing this game I often tried to get the same hanging pawn set-up as White; for example via an-other Keres favourite, 1 d4 ♘f6 2 c4 e6 3 ♘f3 b6 4 e3, continuing 4...♗b7 5 ♗d3 ♗e7 6 0-0 0-0 7 b3 d5 8 ♗b2 c5 9 ♕e2 cxd4 10 exd4 dxc4 11 bxc4.

1 c4 ♘f6 2 ♘f3 e6 3 ♘c3 d5 4 e3

"This game was played in the last round. In order to win first prize I had to go all out for a victory as my nearest rivals were only half a point behind me."

This note of Keres is an example of the fascinating insights one gains from autobiographical games collections. Most players would be focusing on not losing so as to secure at least a share of first place. But Keres shows the quali-ties of a champion by insisting this was a game he had to win.

4...♗e7 5 b3 0-0 6 ♗b2 b6 7 d4 ♗b7 8 ♗d3 dxc4 9 bxc4 c5 10 0-0 cxd4 11 exd4

Establishing a 'hanging pawn' duo on d4 and c4. Although these pawns can become weak they also give White space and attacking chances.

11...♘c6 12 ♕e2 ♖e8

White's last move set a trap: after 12...♘xd4 there follows 13 ♘xd4 ♕xd4 14 ♘d5 ♕c5 15 ♗xf6 ♗xf6 (or 15...gxf6 16 ♕g4+ ♔h8 17 ♕h4 f5 18 ♘xe7 etc)

16 ♕e4, winning a piece.

But Black has a better move in 12...♘b4, when 13 ♗b1 ♗xf3 14 ♕xf3 ♕xd4 15 a3 ♘a6 16 ♕b7 ♗d6! 17 ♕xa6? ♗xh2+ 18 ♔xh2 ♕h4+ 19 ♔g1 ♘g4 gives Black a winning attack. For this reason White would have had to play either 14 gxf3!? ♕xd4 15 ♘e4 or 13 ♖fd1 ♘xd3 14 ♖xd3. And 12 ♖c1 would have been better so as to meet 12...♘b4 with 13 ♗b1 and not shut his rook out of play.

13 ♖fd1 ♖c8 14 ♖ac1 ♕d6

Here, too, 14...♘b4 was interesting. Keres suggested that after 15 ♗b1 ♗xf3 he might play 16 ♕xf3!? ♖xc4 17 d5 exd5 18 a3 ♘c6 19 ♗a2 followed by 20 ♘xd5, but Black has 19...♘d4 (19...♘e5 also seems good) 20 ♕d3 (20 ♕h3 ♖xc3 21 ♖xc3 ♘e2+ is good for Black) 20...♗c5 21 ♗xc4 dxc4 22 ♕xc4 ♘g4 with dangerous threats against White's king. Of course Keres had to analyse this game without the benefit of computer assistance.

15 ♗b1 ♕f4 16 d5!

A move that is typical of hanging

pawn positions, unleashing White's pieces.

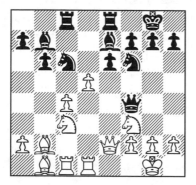

16...exd5 17 cxd5

Here Keres reported having considered the line 17 ♘xd5 ♘xd5 (17...♕h6 18 ♖e1 is just very nice for White) 18 cxd5 ♗f6 19 dxc6 ♖xe2 20 cxb7, but could not calculate all the consequences. So in the end he opted for the relatively simple pawn recapture, which once again is an interesting insight into the thinking of a great player.

17...♘b8

After 17...♗a3 White has 18 dxc6! ♖xe2 19 cxb7 winning, and on 17...♘a5

he can play 18 ♖d4 ♕d6 19 ♕d3, building an imposing position while shutting the knight on a5 out of the game.

18 ♖d4 ♕d6 19 ♖cd1 ♗f8?

Underestimating the strength of White's reply. Black should have played 19...♘bd7, though the position is still very dangerous for him after the reply 20 ♘g5!?.

20 ♘e4! ♘xe4 21 ♖xe4 ♖xe4 22 ♕xe4

22...♕h6

22...g6 23 ♕d4 f6 was a better defence, when White should avoid 24 ♘g5 because of 24...♕xd5, but 24 h4 gives him with a dangerous attack; for example, 24...♖d8 (24...♘d7 25 h5 is strong) 25 ♗d3 ♘d7 (25...♗xd5? 26 ♗c4 wins) 26 h5 ♘e5 27 ♘xe5 ♕xe5 28 ♕xe5 fxe5 29 ♗xe5 wins at least a pawn, since 29...♗xd5? 30 ♗c4 gets the exchange.

23 ♘g5! ♗d6

Now 23...g6 24 ♘xf7! wins immediately.

24 h4! ♘d7 25 ♕f5 ♘f6 26 ♗xf6

With the onset of time trouble White misses a direct win: 26 ♘xf7

♔xf7 27 ♕e6+ ♔f8 28 ♕xd6+ ♔g8 29 ♕e6+ ♔h8 30 d6 and Black's position is hopeless.

26...gxf6

After 26...♕xf6 White plays 27 ♕xh7+ ♔f8 28 ♖e1!, when 28...g6 29 ♘xf7! ♖c7 (or 29...♕xf7 30 ♕h8+ ♕g8 31 ♕f6+ ♕f7 32 ♕xd6+ etc) 30 ♖e8+ ♔xe8 31 ♘xd6+ ♔xd6 32 ♗xg6+ ♔f8 (32...♔d8 33 ♕g8+) 33 ♕h8+ ♔e7 34 ♕g7+ ♔d8 35 ♕g8+ ♔e7 36 ♕f7+ ♔d8 37 ♕e8 is mate.

27 ♘xf7! ♕c1

If Black takes the knight with 27...♔xf7 there follows 28 ♕d7+ ♔g8 (28...♗e7 29 d6 wins) 29 ♕xd6 ♖c1 30 ♕b8+ ♗c8 31 ♖xc1 ♕xc1+ 32 ♔h2 ♕xb1 33 ♕xc8+ ♔f7 34 d6 and White wins the queen endgame.

28 ♕xh7+ ♔f8 29 ♘xd6 ♕xd1+ 30 ♔h2 ♕xd5 31 ♘xb7

With two minor pieces for a rook and an ongoing attack White is now winning.

31...♕e5+ 32 g3 ♖c7 33 ♕h8+ ♔f7 34 h5 ♖xb7 35 ♕h7+ ♔e6 36 ♕xb7 ♕xh5+ 37 ♔g2 1-0

One Hundred Selected Games (Mikhail Botvinnik)

Mikhail Botvinnik is not the most glamorous of chess idols but he was my hero during my teenage years. He was World Chess Champion from 1948 until 1963 with just two short breaks when Vassily Smyslov and Mikhail Tal won matches from him, only to lose the return match the following year.

While being very much a complete player in just about every aspect of his game, Botvinnik's style was particularly distinguished by great strategic depth. This first volume of his games features those up to 1946, two years before he became World Champion, and at that time his play was quite sharp. One particularly memorable game for me was his win against Alatortsev in the Queen's Gambit Declined, as I managed to use this scheme quite a lot in my junior days.

> ### Game 38
> ### M.Botvinnik-V.Alatortsev
> ### Leningrad 1934
> *Queen's Gambit Declined*

1 d4 e6 2 c4 d5 3 ♘f3 ♗e7

A favourite move order of Alatortsev which gained more popularity against 3 ♘c3. Here it is little more than a harmless transposition of moves.

4 ♘c3 ♘f6 5 ♗g5 0-0 6 e3 a6?!

These days Black usually plays

6...♘bd7 and waits for 7 ♖c1 before playing 7...a6. The game move is inaccurate because White can adopt a plan in which ...a7-a6 is a waste of time.

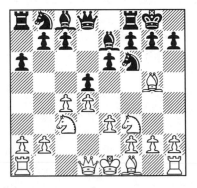

7 cxd5 exd5 8 ♗d3 c6?!

Black's position would still have been playable after the immediate 8...♘bd7, when 9 ♕c2 ♖e8 10 g4 can be met by 10...♘f8. After 8...c6 it's a very different story, as Black is missing a crucial tempo.

9 ♕c2 ♘bd7 10 g4!

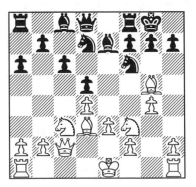

A powerful and surprising move which pinpoints the problem with Black's 6...a6.

10...♘xg4?

In a difficult position Black plays the weakest available line. But in fairness he is also struggling after other possibilities. For example:

a) There is no time for 10...♖e8 because of 11 ♗xf6 followed by 12 g5, winning the h7-pawn and demolishing Black's kingside.

b) 10...h6 11 ♗f4 leaves White threatening g4-g5, smashing open the kingside, while 11...♘xg4? 12 ♖g1 leads to a winning attack for White.

c) 10...g6 was a better try, though with the pawn on g6 rather than g7 Black's king position would be quite vulnerable.

11 ♗xh7+ ♔h8 12 ♗f4

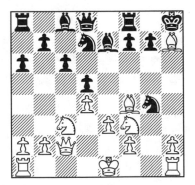

12...♘df6

Kasparov points out that after 12...g6 13 ♗xg6! fxg6 14 ♕xg6 ♘gf6 (14...♘df6 runs into 15 h3, while 14...♖xf4 15 exf4 ♘f8 is strongly met by 16 ♕h5+ ♘h7 17 ♖g1 ♘gf6 18 ♘e5 threatening 19 ♘f7 mate) 15 ♘g5 ♕e8 16 ♕h6+ ♔g8 17 ♖g1 White has a winning attack.

13 ♗d3 ♘h5

It's not easy to find a decent alternative.

14 h3 ♘gf6 15 ♗e5 ♘g8 16 0-0-0 ♘h6 17 ♖dg1 ♗e6 18 ♕e2 ♗f5?

This blunder hastens the end. Black should have tried 18...♘f6, but then 19 ♘g5 would have been very unpleasant.

19 ♗xf5 ♘xf5 20 ♘h4! 1-0

Resistance is futile; for example, 20 ♘h4 ♘xh4 (or 20...♗xh4 21 ♕xh5+ ♔g8 22 ♕xf5) 21 ♕xh5+ ♔g8 22 ♖xg7 mate.

The book also contains several articles by Botvinnik, one of which details his famous methods of preparation.

Nimzowitsch: A Reappraisal
(by Raymond Keene)

Aaron Nimzowitsch is widely regarded as one of the giants of chess strategy, but I found his own books very difficult to read or understand. *My System* was in fact inspired by a book of the same name by the Danish athlete, Jørgen Peter Müller. Nimzowitsch was much taken with the athlete's exercises (he mentioned them in his book on the Carlsbad 1929 tournament book) and decided to produce his own system.

Raymond Keene's book explains Nimzowitsch's thinking and influence on the modern game in a far more lucid and accessible way. I found it immensely helpful and took it just about everywhere with me for several months.

The Art of the Middle Game
(Paul Keres and Alexander Kotov)

This is essential reading for anyone who is serious about improving; there are just so many valuable insights in this book. But there is one chapter in particular which I believe has immense value, the one by Keres on defending difficult positions.

Here's a taste of what you can expect; it is really worth its weight in gold to anyone who aspires to improve.

"However hopeless the situation appears to be there yet always exists the possibility of putting up a stubborn resistance. And it is the player's task to find these opportunities and make the best of them. When the player with the upper hand is continually confronted by new problems, when, at every moment, one renders the win as difficult as possible, then it is likely that his powers will eventually weaken and he may make some mistake."

In the following game Keres practiced what he preached and even managed to swindle the great David Bronstein:

1 e4 e5 2 ♘f3 ♘c6 3 ♗b5 a6 4 ♗a4 ♘f6 5 0-0 ♗e7 6 ♖e1 b5 7 ♗b3 d6 8 c3 0-0 9 h3 ♘a5 10 ♗c2 c5 11 d4 ♕c7

Keres would later pioneer the variation with 11...♘d7 which would come to be named after him.

12 ♘bd2 cxd4 13 cxd4 ♘c6 14 ♘b3

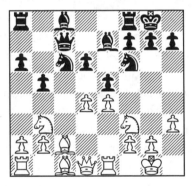

14...♗b7?!

Black's position becomes very passive after this, especially when his knight has to retreat to d8. He should play 14...a5 instead; for example, 15 ♗e3 (15 d5 ♘b4 gives Black excellent counterplay) 15...a4 16 ♘bd2 ♗d7 17 ♖c1 ♕b7 18 ♘f1 ♖fe8 19 ♘g3 ♗d8 20 ♗b1 h6 21 ♖e2 ♗b6 22 dxe5 ♘xe5! 23 ♘h4 ♗xe3 24 ♖xe3 d5 kept the balance in P.Leko-V.Bologan, Dortmund 2004.

15 ♗g5 h6 16 ♗h4 ♘h5 17 d5 ♘d8 18 ♗xe7 ♕xe7 19 ♘fd4!

An ingenious way to bring the knight to f5.

19...♘f4 20 ♘f5 ♕f6 21 ♖e3 ♔h7 22 a4 bxa4 23 ♖xa4 ♗c8 24 ♖b4

White is clearly better here because of the vast superiority in the placement of his pieces. The main problem for Black is the cramping effect of that pawn on d5 which severely restricts his knight on d8.

24...♘b7 25 ♖c3 g6 26 ♘e3 a5 27 ♖b6 ♕d8 28 ♘c4 ♖a7 29 ♘c1 ♕g5 30 ♖g3 ♕e7 31 ♘e2 ♘xe2+ 32 ♕xe2 ♖d8 33 ♖a3 ♗d7 34 ♕e3 ♖c8 35 ♗d3

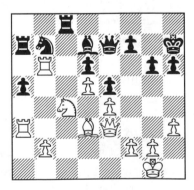

Here's what Keres had to say about this position:

"Black's plight is wretched in the extreme. White has, it is true, no plus in material, but his pieces command the whole board and it seems to be merely a matter of time before Black's position collapses. A cramped position is not in itself a disaster, but if, in addition, one has no prospects of counterplay, then the situation usually becomes quickly hopeless. This, too, is the case here. When one considers Black's plausible moves then it soon becomes apparent that he can scarcely move anything without incurring a speedy loss. The queen and the knight are tied to the pawn on d6; the rook on a7 must protect the knight, and the bishop on d7 has only one move, to e8. One can hardly think of a more hopeless situation, but even in such a position one ought to try to find some satisfactory method of defence.

"Of course the reader will understand that I am not attempting to prove that Black's position is to be held by good defensive moves. That would be an insoluble problem, since White has a won game. Instead, the aim in this example is to demonstrate that even a position that is ripe for resignation can, despite everything, afford defensive possibilities that make the opponent's task more difficult. The game's final outcome depended less on my good defence, since in reality nothing like this is to be found, than on the psychological effect that my obstinate 'never surrender' tactics had on my opponent. These represent, however, the only kind of tactics that one can employ in such positions.

"Now, however, back to the game. What can Black try in the diagram position? Naturally, nothing. But this does not mean that he should wander planlessly to and fro, waiting to see how White will consummate his advantage for a win. In every position, no matter how bad it may be, there always exist chances for small finesses, which one must employ whenever possible. It should never be forgotten that, in a superior position, one is always looking for a clear way to win. Quite often small advantages are despised, since one wants to obtain more out of the position. This factor, easily understood from the psychological angle, must be utilized, since thereby one can often embark on variations which one would never have been wont to try in equal positions. Psychological methods of warfare are the only possibilities in such positions."

35...♗e8! 36 b4!

If 36 ♘xd6 ♘xd6 37 ♖xd6 ♕xd6 38 ♕xa7, then 38...♕b4! would give Black some counterplay.

36...a4 37 ♔h2 ♖aa8 38 ♗e2 ♖c7 39 b5 ♕d8 40 ♖a2

Black is making it as hard as possible for his opponent to score the full point. Here White cannot play 40 f4? because of 40...exf4 41 ♕xf4 ♖xc4 42 ♖xb7 ♖c7.

40...♔g7 41 ♖c6

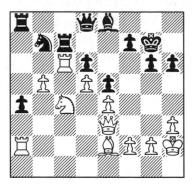

A very strong sealed move which gives White a winning position. The only problem was that it cost 35 minutes on the clock.

41...♖b8

After 41...♗xc6 42 dxc6 ♘c5 White would have 43 ♘xe5.

42 ♖d2!

Bronstein used even more time on this move. According to Keres he had been visibly shocked by the move 41...♖b8. On 42 ♖xa4 there is 42...♗xc6 43 dxc6 ♘c5 44 ♖a5 ♘e6, when the knight can plant itself on the d4-square.

42...h5 43 ♖d1

According to Keres 43 ♕c3! would have been decisive (the threats include ♘xd6, ♘xe5 and f2-f4); but the presence of this winning line takes nothing away from Black's resourceful defence which made things as difficult as possible for White.

43...♔g8 44 ♔g1 ♔h7 45 ♕a3 ♕e7 46 ♕xa4?

More of Bronstein's thinking time went on 46 ♘xd6 ♗xc6 47 dxc6 ♘xd6

48 ♕xd6 (48 ♖xd6 ♖d8 49 ♖d3 ♕xa3 50 ♖xa3 ♖d4 and ...♖b4 would make it tough for White) 48...♕xd6 49 ♖xd6 a3 50 ♖d2 ♖a7.

But 46 ♕c3! would again have been very strong.

46...♘c5

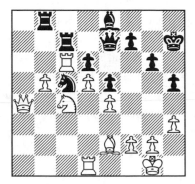

47 ♕c2?!

White should have played 47 ♕a5, after which 47...♗xc6 (47...♖a7! is better) 48 dxc6 ♘xe4 49 ♗f3 is very good for White.

47...♗xc6! 48 dxc6 ♖xb5! 49 ♘xd6

Missing a draw with 49 ♘e3! ♖b8 50 ♘d5 ♕d8 51 ♘xc7 ♕xc7 52 ♗c4. After the text White has to be very careful.

49...♖b6 50 ♗b5?

A fatal mistake in time trouble. There was still a way for White to hold the game: 50 ♕xc5 ♖cxc6 51 ♕xb6 ♖xb6 52 ♘c8 ♕c5 53 ♘xb6 ♕xb6 and the pawns are restricted to one side of the board.

50...♘e6 51 ♗a4 ♘d4 52 ♕c5 ♖bxc6! 53 ♗xc6 ♖xc6 0-1

Here White lost on time.

Together with the section on defence in Lasker's *Manual* (book no.3 above), this has to be one of the most useful things I have ever seen written about chess and has helped me pull off many fightbacks in my own games. Here's an example from my best ever tournament win:

> ### Game 40
> ### M.Hennigan-N.Davies
> Wrexham 1994
> *Scotch Game*

1 e4 e5 2 ᐃf3 ᐃc6 3 d4 exd4 4 ᐃxd4 ♗c5 5 ᐃxc6 bxc6

5...♕f6 is the book move, but I wanted to go my own way.

6 ♗d3 ᐃe7

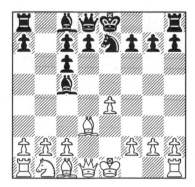

An interesting possibility was 6...♕h4 7 0-0 ᐃf6 with some annoying counterplay for Black.

7 ᐃd2

A couple of strong players tried this line after me and their opponents both played 7 0-0. The games went 7...0-0 8

ᐃd2 d6 9 ᐃb3 ♗b6, and now 10 ♗g5 ♗e6 11 c3 h6 12 ♗h4 g5 13 ♗g3 f5 14 exf5 ᐃxf5 was fine for Black in M.Kobalia-A.Lastin, Russian Championship, Samara 2000, while 10 c4 ♗e6 11 ♗e2 ᐃg6 12 ᐃd4 ♕h4 13 f4 ᐃe5! was even slightly better for Black in R.Reinaldo Castineira-G.Giorgadze, Mondariz 2000.

7...ᐃg6

Making room for the bishop to drop back to e7, but this leaves Black rather passively placed. In retrospect I should probably have just played 7...d6 and met 8 ᐃb3 ♗b6 9 c4 with 9...♗e6 10 c5?! ♗xb3 etc.

8 ᐃb3 ♗e7 9 0-0 0-0 10 f4 d6 11 ♕h5

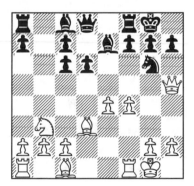

It was around here that I realized what a difficult position I had found myself in, with White's pieces ready to charge forward on the kingside. I resolved to make life as difficult for him as possible.

11...♖e8 12 ᐃd4 ♗d7 13 ᐃf3 ♕c8

This was motivated by the desire to get White to commit himself with f4-f5 (he must do something to prevent the threat of 14...♗g4). Unfortunately it does not achieve very much after White advances his f-pawn. 13...♕b8 is probably better, so as to activate the queen via b6.

14 f5 ♘f8

In an increasingly unpleasant position I wanted to make it as hard as possible for White to find a clear line of action. After 14...♘e5?! 15 ♘xe5 dxe5 16 ♗c4 ♖f8 17 ♖f3, followed by 18 ♖h3, White would get a winning attack.

15 g4 ♖b8 16 ♗d2

The immediate 16 ♗c4 may well be stronger, but there too Black is not without his chances. I was intending to play 16...d5 17 exd5 ♖b4, when 18 b3 ♗f6 19 ♖b1 g6 starts to mix it up.

16...♗f6 17 ♗c4?!

Amazingly Black can take the initiative after this. 17 ♗c3 looks better, just exchanging off a defender and not worrying too much about the doubled c-pawns.

17...g6 18 ♕h6 d5! 19 exd5 ♖e4

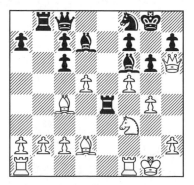

Hitting both c4 and g4. The game is rapidly approaching boiling point.

20 fxg6 hxg6 21 ♘g5 ♖xg4+ 22 ♔h1 ♗g7

After agreeing with my previous five moves, *Fritz 12* prefers 22...♗f5 here. Certainly it's a lot safer than allowing the following queen sacrifice.

23 ♕xg7+ ♔xg7 24 ♖xf7+ ♔h6 25 ♘e6+ g5 26 ♖f6+

At first *Fritz* wanted White to go into an exchange-down endgame by playing 26 ♘xf8 ♖xf8 27 ♖xf8 ♖xf8, but that option would hardly be to a humanoid's taste.

26...♘g6 27 ♗d3 ♕g8 28 ♘xg5

Here, too, *Fritz* felt White could do better, this time with 28 h3; but after 28...♖g3 29 ♖xg6+ ♕xg6 30 ♗xg6 ♔xg6 White is again left with a miserable endgame.

28...♕xd5+ 29 ♘f3+

29...♔h5

I cannot remember why I thought the king had to advance. 29...♔h7 would have been much simpler.

30 h3?

In time trouble White makes the losing error. 30 ♖e1 was a much better try, when the position is still very difficult.

30...♖g3 31 ♗e2 ♖e8 32 ♖f7 ♖xh3+ 33 ♔g1 ♖xe2 0-1

Zoom 001: Zero Hour to the Operation of Opening Models (Steffen Zeuthen and Bent Larsen)

A lot of people have not heard of this book, which is still being published by the Skakhuset in Denmark but is only available if you buy it from them. I was first put on to the value of this work by International Master Danny Kopec.

ZOOM stands for 'ZERO Hour to the OPERATION of OPENING MODELS', the authors' aim being to help the reader master a particular strategic pattern which involves one (or both) sides adopting a kingside fianchetto and then playing on the d- and c-files.

This is one of the books that has had a great influence on me throughout my chess career. I think that developing a good understanding of particular patterns is far more important than attempting to study the latest games and find 'theoretical novelties'. A new move rarely has great significance and novelties are often worse than the known continuations, but understanding is a continually acting factor which can guide a player throughout a game.

As a result of studying *ZOOM 001* I have always been attracted to ZOOM formations, and the Catalan and Grün-

feld have been great point scorers for me. I am also in great company as many top Grandmasters have played these positions throughout their careers. The names which come immediately to mind are those of Victor Korchnoi, Vassily Smyslov, Rafael Vaganian, Bent Larsen, Zoltan Ribli and Leonid Stein.

Here's one of my games with a ZOOM set-up, again from Wrexham 1994.

Game 41
N.Davies-R.Dive
Wrexham 1994
Catalan Opening

1 d4 ♘f6 2 c4 e6 3 g3 c6

A slightly bizarre move; after ...d7-d5 it would be completely illogical for White to exchange with c4xd5 because that would free Black's bishop on c8. So why prepare it?

4 ♘f3 ♗e7 5 ♗g2 0-0 6 0-0 d5 7 ♕c2 b5

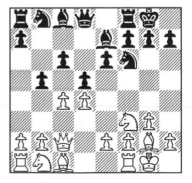

Not a bad idea in itself, but it needs

to be followed up correctly. If Black wanted to adopt a Stonewall formation he should have done it now with 7...♘e4 followed by 8...f5.

8 c5 ♘e4

This is asking too much of the position. Black has a good option here in 8...a5!?; for example, 9 ♘bd2 ♗a6!? 10 e4 dxe4 (10...♘bd7 is also possible, letting White push on to e5) 11 ♘xe4 ♘xe4 12 ♕xe4 b4! 13 ♖d1 ♗c4 and with his bishop coming to d5, Black had a very reasonable position in L.Bruzon Bautista-R.Hernandez Onna, Santa Clara 2004.

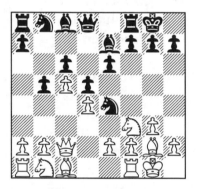

9 ♘e5 f5 10 ♘d2 a5 11 ♘xe4 dxe4

11...fxe4 is also good for White after 12 f3 exf3 13 ♗xf3, since Black will have trouble developing his knight to d7 without misplacing his rook via 13...♖a6.

12 ♖d1 ♕e8

It starts to become apparent that the weakness of the c6-pawn gives Black serious problems with his development. This was the drawback to playing both 7...b5 and 8...♘e4, which

White now exacerbates by opening the position.

13 f3 exf3 14 ♗xf3 ♗b7 15 a4

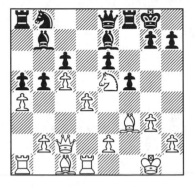

Creating a new weakness: the c4-square. This proves to be a great post for White's knight.

15...b4 16 ♕b3

Now the e6-pawn is marked out as a weakness.

16...♗d8 17 ♘c4 ♗c7 18 ♗f4!

The exchange of Black's dark-squared bishop leaves him facing a strategic nightmare. His position has more holes than Swiss cheese.

18...♗xf4 19 gxf4 ♖a7 20 ♔h1

Fritz later pointed out an immediate and brutal win of two pawns with 20 ♘xa5 ♖xa5 21 ♕xb4 ♖a7 22 ♕b6!, when Black must give up his bishop on b7. Fortunately I missed it, as the combination I manage to pull off in the game features a very unusual theme.

20...♕e7 21 ♘e5 ♗a8 22 ♖g1

With Black tied to the defence of his c-pawn I set about attacking him on the other side of the board. There is not really much he can do about it.

22...罝f6 23 罝g5 含h8 24 罝ag1 罝h6 25 罝1g3 嶜e8 26 嶜e3

Preparing to triple my major pieces on the g-file.

26...嶜c8 27 嶜g1 g6

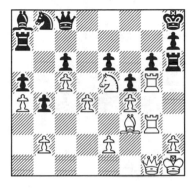

28 奧h5!

No doubt White can win without this, but it seemed like too good an opportunity to miss. The theme of sacrificing on an empty square in this way is very unusual. Black has to deal with the threat of 29 奧xg6, but in taking the bishop he loses by force.

28...罝xh5

On 28...嶜d8 there would follow 29 奧xg6 hxg6 30 罝xg6 嶜d5+ 31 勾f3 and Black gets mated.

29 勾xg6+! hxg6 30 罝xg6 嶜d7 31 罝g8+ 含h7 32 罝h8+! 1-0

The final sacrifice, forcing mate. After 32...含xh8 there follows 33 罝g8+ 含h7 34 嶜g6 mate.

Pawn Power in Chess
(Hans Kmoch)

Other players will have their own favourites but a few of these books should be on everyone's list. *Pawn Power in Chess* is just such a book and has helped both me and many of my students make a breakthrough with their game.

Knowing what to do with pawns, rather than just the pieces, is what distinguishes a strategist from a tactician and this book teaches exactly how to do that. Kmoch's homemade terminology can take a bit of getting used to, but once you get over that this book is pure gold.

The following game was played just after my first reading of Kmoch's masterpiece and featured the kind of pawn play that was previously quite alien to me.

Game 42
N.Davies-P.Motwani
London 1982
Modern Defence

1 d4 g6 2 e4 奧g7 3 勾f3 d6 4 c3

If you play the Modern Defence enough you learn that this is an unpleasant line to face. White immediately shuts down the a1-h8 diagonal, so as to neutralize Black's dangerous king's bishop, and relies on having a small space advantage in the centre.

4...勾d7?!

This is now known to be difficult for Black, who will find it hard to force White to dissolve his central pawn duo (either with d4-d5 or d4xe5). My own preference has been for 4...♞c6 followed by ...e7-e5 with far more pressure against d4.

5 ♗d3 e5 6 0-0 ♞gf6 7 ♖e1 0-0 8 ♗g5 h6 9 ♗h4 c6?!

Rather than weaken the d6-square like this it's probably better to play 9...b6 and 10...♗b7.

10 ♞bd2 ♛c7

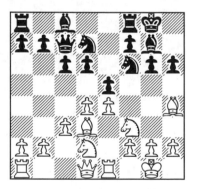

11 ♗f1

This may look very quiet, but White is clearing the d-file so that his queen can invade the d6-square.

11...b6

After this White's strategy proceeds

without a hitch. Perhaps Black should have played 11...♞b6, so as to exchange White's knight off should it land on c4.

12 ♞c4 ♗b7

White can also meet 12...b5 with 13 dxe5 dxe5 14 ♛d6! and a clear advantage.

13 dxe5 dxe5 14 ♛d6!

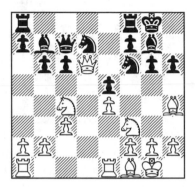

The exchange of queens is the most effective way for White to pursue his initiative, as Black's queen is a vital defender of the dark squares in his camp.

14...♖ac8 15 ♖ad1 ♛xd6 16 ♞xd6 ♖c7 17 ♞xb7

Trading the knight for another advantage: the bishop pair.

17...♖xb7 18 ♞d2

Bringing the other knight towards the queenside while unblocking the f-pawn. This makes f2-f3 and ♗h4-f2 possible, bringing the bishop on h4 back into the game.

18...♞c5 19 f3 ♞h5 20 ♞c4 ♖c7 21 ♖d1

21 ♗f2 might have been more precise, preventing Black's next. In any case there will be no easy end to Black's suffering.

21...b5 22 ♘a5 ♖fc8 23 ♖ed1 ♗f6 24 ♗f2

White could have cashed in immediately with 24 ♗xf6! ♘xf6 25 ♖d8+ ♔g7 26 ♖xc8 ♖xc8 27 ♖d6; for example, 27...♘a4 28 ♖xc6 ♖xc6 29 ♘xc6 a6 30 ♘xe5 ♘xb2 31 c4 b4 32 ♘c6 wins easily in the endgame. That's not to say that 24 ♗f2 is bad, since White still has very strong pressure.

24...♗e7 25 g3

Introducing the possibility of ♗f1-h3 while keeping Black's knight on h5 out of f4.

25...♘f6 26 ♖c2

And now 'Pawn Power' makes itself felt; White is aiming for c3-c4. I am not sure this would have occurred to me a couple of years earlier.

26...♖b8 27 a3 ♘a4 28 b3 ♘b6 29 b4 ♔g7 30 c4!

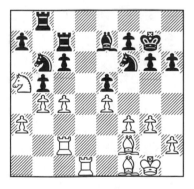

A very powerful pawn lever, straight from *Pawn Power in Chess*. Black's position collapses very quickly.

30...bxc4 31 ♗xc4 ♘xc4 32 ♘xc4 ♖b5 33 ♗e1 ♘d7 34 ♗c3 ♗f6

A better attempt to confuse matters

lay in 34...c5, though after 35 a4 cxb4 (35...♖bb7 36 b5 f6 37 ♘a5 is horrific) 36 axb5 ♖xc4 37 ♖xd7 ♗c5+ 38 ♔f1 bxc3 39 ♖c7 Black is totally tied up.

35 ♖cd2 ♘f8 36 ♖d6 ♘e6 37 ♖d7 ♖xd7

Going to his doom relatively meekly. *Fritz* pointed out the amazing 37...♖d5!?, but White can keep control with 38 exd5 ♖xd7 39 d6.

38 ♖xd7 ♘d4 39 ♔f2 ♖b8 40 f4

Undermining the position of the knight on d4, after which Black's game falls apart.

40...♘b5 41 ♗xe5 ♗xe5 42 ♘xe5 ♘xa3 43 ♖xf7+ ♔g8 44 ♖xa7 ♘b5 45 ♖d7 ♘c3 46 ♖d4 ♖b6 47 ♖c4 1-0

The fall of a third pawn (c6) is way too much.

Case History: Nigel Colter

Nigel Colter is a great example of how Kmoch's *Pawn Power in Chess* can help an over-40 player improve. When he came to me in 2003 he was languishing down around 1600; now his playing strength is in excess of 2000 with the grade still lagging behind a bit.

How did he do it?

Essentially Nigel switched from playing for short-term tactics to working on pawn structures and strategy. Besides studying Kmoch's book he did some work on endgames and started playing some solid openings.

Here are four of Nigel's games showing his play before and after. And I think he has the potential to improve further still.

Game 43
N.Colter-T.Donnelly
London 2004
Queen's Pawn Opening

1 d4 c5 2 dxc5

Black's last move prevented Nigel from adopting his then favourite opening, the Tromp (1...♘f6 2 ♗g5); and without a solid grounding in pawn structures he was reticent about taking the space with 2 d5.

2...e6 3 ♘d2

Now Black is doing quite well. 3 ♗e3 is more testing, making it difficult for Black to recover his pawn.

3...♗xc5 4 ♘b3 ♗b6 5 e4

Getting a kind of Sicilian structure, but with White's pieces far more passively placed than they would be in a real Sicilian.

5...♘e7 6 ♕g4?!

Black can meet this with a good developing move and the queen is exposed here. 6 ♘f3 was better, simply aiming to get the pieces out. White should not be worse here, providing he plays sensibly.

6...0-0 7 ♗d3 f5

Initiating active counterplay. Not only is the f2-pawn in the firing line from Black's rook on f8 and bishop on b6, he now gets a dangerous central pawn majority.

8 exf5 ♘xf5 9 ♘f3 d5

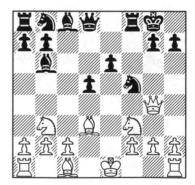

10 ♗g5?!

Piece play alone does not meet the demands of this position. White should have played 10 0-0, followed by c2-c4, trying to break up Black's pawn centre while it is still possible.

10...♕e8 11 0-0-0 ♘c6 12 ♔b1?

Black's reply is simple but incredibly strong. White had to try something like 12 ♗xf5 ♖xf5 13 ♗e3, getting some pieces off while temporarily holding up Black's d- and e-pawns. In this way he would still be in the game.

12...e5!

Of course! Suddenly White faces the threat of ...e5-e4, not to mention veiled threats against his queen from the bishop on c8.

13 ♗xf5 ♗xf5 14 ♕g3 ♕e6

14...♘b4 is even stronger; for example, after 15 ♘e1 (15 ♖d2 ♕a4 gives Black a winning attack) 15...♗xf2! 16 ♕xf2 ♗xc2+ 17 ♕xc2 ♘xc2 18 ♘xc2 ♕g6 the three discoordinated pieces are no match for Black's queen and protected passed pawns.

15 ♖d2

15 ♖he1 was better, though still horrible for White: 15...h6 16 ♗c1 ♖ac8.

15...h6

16 ♗xh6?

Desperation; White gets nothing for the piece.

16...♕xh6 17 ♖xd5 ♗xc2+! 18 ♔a1

18 ♔xc2 ♘b4+ picks up the rook on d5.

18...♗xb3 19 axb3 e4

Black's initiative keeps coming even after the win of a piece.

20 ♖d6 ♖f6 21 ♖xf6 ♕xf6 22 ♘g5 0-1

Game 44
E.Bromillow-N.Colter
Middlesex Open 2003
Dutch Defence

1 d4 e6 2 ♘f3 f5 3 g3 ♗e7

Black's move order is somewhat odd, but there doesn't seem to be too much wrong with it apart from the loss of a few options. The immediate 3...♘f6 is the usual move.

4 ♗g2 d6 5 b3 ♘f6 6 0-0 0-0 7 c4 ♘e4 8 ♘fd2

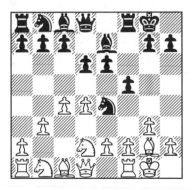

Not mentioned in Simon Williams' book on the Classical Dutch which came out the same year. Black's reply looks pretty good.

8...d5 9 ♘xe4 fxe4

Here, however, there's a case for 9...dxe4!? in order to put pressure on White's d-pawn. Then the game might have continued 10 ♘c3 ♘c6 11 d5 ♗f6 12 dxc6 ♗xc3 13 ♕xd8 ♖xd8 14 ♗g5 ♖d6 15 cxb7 ♗xb7 with approximate equality.

10 ♗a3 ♗xa3 11 ♘xa3 ♕e7 12 ♘b5 c6 13 ♘c3

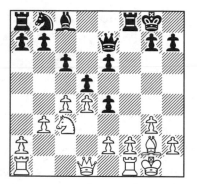

13...b6?!

Thus far things have been going well enough for Black, but this is a mistake. The correct move was 13...♘d7 when 14 f3 could be answered by 14...exf3 15 exf3 dxc4 16 bxc4 e5, freeing Black's game and giving him adequate counterplay.

14 f3 ♕g5?!

Threatening ...♕e3+, but making matters worse by losing more time. Black should be trying to develop via 14...exf3 15 ♖xf3 ♖xf3 16 exf3 ♘d7, which is hardly pleasant but may not be too bad.

15 ♕c1 ♕xc1 16 ♖axc1 exf3 17 ♗xf3 ♗b7 18 ♗g4

18 cxd5 exd5 19 e4 was also strong.

18...♖e8 19 ♖f2 ♘d7 20 cxd5 cxd5 21 ♘b5 ♘f6

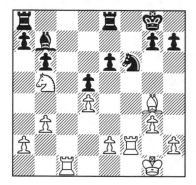

22 ♗h3

22 ♖c7! was even stronger; for example, 22...♗a6 23 ♘d6 (23 ♖xf6 gxf6 24 ♘d6 is also good) 23...♘xg4 24 ♖ff7 ♘f6 25 ♖xg7+ ♔h8 26 ♘xe8 ♖xe8 27 ♖gf7 ♘e4 28 ♖xh7+ etc.

22...♘e4

22...♖e7 would have been more tenacious, though it still looks good for White after 23 ♖c7! ♔f8 24 ♗xe6 ♖xe6 25 ♖xb7.

23 ♖ff1 ♖e7 24 ♘c7 ♘g5

Desperation.

25 ♘xa8 ♘xh3+ 26 ♔g2 ♘g5 27 ♖c7

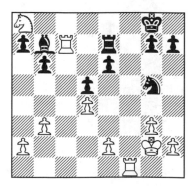

Simplifying into a position where the outcome is beyond doubt.

27...♖xc7 28 ♘xc7 e5 29 e3 exd4 30 exd4 ♗c8 31 ♖c1 ♗f5 32 ♘b5 ♗e4+ 33 ♔f2 1-0

Game 45
R.Parsons-N.Colter
Harrow 2009
Caro-Kann Defence

---

1 e4 c6

Since we started working together Nigel has switched from a tricky line of the Scandinavian to solid play with the Caro-Kann. To a certain extent these two openings are similar, for example many lines produce the same pawn structure. But the Caro is a higher quality defence with a distinct absence of tricks.

2 ♘f3 d5 3 exd5 cxd5 4 ♗b5+

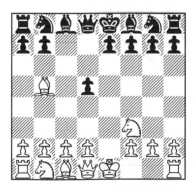

The Caro is not a popular choice at club level and it looks as if White is on his own resources already. His play here is not good, because exchanging light-squared bishops makes it easy for Black to know where his pawns belong.

4...♗d7 5 ♗xd7+ ♘xd7 6 ♘c3

Another dubious move. In pawn structures like this White should play d2-d4 and c2-c3 and then put the queen's knight on d2, from where it is within relatively easy reach of e5 (the outpost on the half-open e-file).

6...♘gf6 7 d3 e6 8 0-0 ♗d6 9 ♗g5 0-0 10 ♕d2 a6

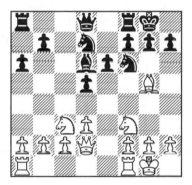

Not just preventing ♘c3-b5 ideas, Black is preparing to expand on the queenside with ...b7-b5, so that he can ultimately extend his control of the half-open c-file with ...b5-b4. This is a typical strategy for 'minority attack' positions, but such knowledge is rarely acquired by club level players.

11 a3 ♕c7 12 h3 ♖fc8 13 ♖fe1 b5

Logically expanding on the queenside. Black is already better.

14 ♕e2 b4 15 axb4 ♗xb4 16 d4?

Strategic suicide. White really has to play 16 ♗d2 in this position, preventing the discombobulation of his pawn structure.

16...♗xc3 17 bxc3 ♛c4!

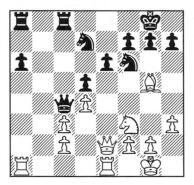

A classy decision by Black. With the queens off the only important factors will be White's doubled c-pawns, the outpost on c4 and Black's passed a-pawn. While the queens were still on White might hope to get some counterplay against the black king.

18 ♛xc4 ♖xc4 19 ♗d2 ♘e4 20 ♖e3 h5

Not strictly necessary, but not bad either.

21 ♗e1 ♚f8 22 ♘e5 ♘xe5 23 dxe5 a5

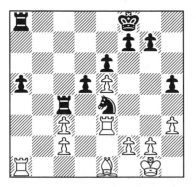

Black's a-pawn will be decisive.

24 f3 ♘c5 25 g4 hxg4 26 hxg4 a4 27 ♗d2 ♘d7

More wonderfully logical positional play. Nigel sees that the knight is best placed on the c4-outpost and sets about repositioning it.

28 ♖a3 ♘b6 29 ♚g2 ♖cc8 30 ♖e2 ♘c4 31 ♖a1 ♘xd2

Cashing in his monster knight to make the first material gains.

32 ♖xd2 ♖xc3 33 ♚f2 a3 34 ♖a2 ♖b8 35 ♚e2 ♖b2 36 ♖a1 a2 37 f4

37...f6

The final stage is to activate Black's king. I might have preferred to do this without the ...f7-f6-pawn lever, but this is largely a matter of taste.

38 exf6 gxf6 39 g5 fxg5 40 fxg5 ♚g7 41 ♚f2 ♚g6 42 ♚e2 ♚xg5 43 ♚f2 ♖cxc2 44 ♖xc2 ♖xc2+ 45 ♚e3 ♚f5 46 ♖f1+ ♚e5 47 ♖a1 ♖h2 48 ♖f1 ♖h3+ 49 ♚e2 ♖a3 50 ♚d2 a1♛ 0-1

> ## Game 46
> ### N.Colter-C.Kreuzer
> South Herts Major 2007
> *Trompowsky Opening*

1 d4 ♘f6 2 ♗g5

Nigel was still playing the Trompowsky at this time, but with a much greater emphasis on strategy and structure.

2...e6 3 ♘d2 d5 4 e3 c5 5 c3 ♘c6 6 f4

This is one of the advantage of delaying ♘g1-f3: White can often try to set up a Stonewall structure with his bishop outside the pawn chain.

6...♗e7 7 ♗d3 ♘d7 8 ♗xe7 ♕xe7

To some extent the exchange of bishops has freed Black's position, but the one he is left with is hemmed in by his own pawns. This becomes more serious after his later 11...f5.

9 ♘gf3 0-0 10 0-0 ♖e8 11 ♘e5 f5 12 ♘df3 ♘cxe5 13 fxe5 g5?!

This looks very risky. A much simpler move was 13...b6, with what looks like a solid position for Black.

14 ♔h1 g4

This is not so much an attacking move as a defensive measure against White opening the kingside, though I am not entirely sure it was meant that way. Thanks to the cramping effect of his pawn on e5 (which denies Black's

pieces access to f6) it is White who has the chances on the kingside.

15 ♘g1 ♕g5 16 ♕d2 h5 17 ♕f2 ♖f8 18 ♕f4

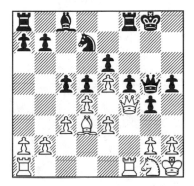

I am not sure I would have played it like this, but White's willingness to go into an endgame shows a touch of class. Another way to play was 18 h4!? ♕g7 19 g3, intending ♘g1-e2-f4. White could also consider the transfer of his knight to f4 without first closing the kingside.

18...♕xf4 19 exf4 cxd4?

A strategic blunder; Black should keep the queenside closed for as long as he possibly can.

20 cxd4 ♘b6 21 b3!

Simply taking c4 away from Black's knight.

21...♗d7 22 ♖ac1 ♖ac8 23 ♖c5!

Occupying the outpost on the open file. If Black takes it then after 24 dxc5 White's knight will come to e2 and then d4.

23...♖c6 24 ♖xc6 ♗xc6 25 ♖c1 ♔f7 26 ♘e2 ♖c8 27 ♔g1 ♔e7

27...♗d7 would have been better,

though White continues to press after 28 ♖c5!. I am not sure White can win this position against the 'best defence', but it will be difficult for Black in practice with the c-file to protect and the weakness on h5.

28 ♔f2 h4 29 h3

29...g3+?!

Leaving himself with serious obligations on the kingside. 29...gxh3 was better, so that after 30 gxh3 ♘d7 he could protect his one vulnerable kingside pawn by bringing the knight to f8 and g6.

30 ♔e3

30...♗e8?

Losing. He should still bring the knight to g6, but then 30...♘d7 31 ♘g1 ♘f8 32 ♘f3 ♘g6 33 ♗e2 prepares further torture via ♘f3-g5 and ♗e2-h5, threatening to exchange the h4-pawn's defender. And if that one goes g3 will be weak as well.

31 ♖xc8 ♘xc8 32 ♘g1 ♗h5 33 ♗e2

Presumably Black had missed this move. With the exchange of bishops there's nothing to stop White's knight from coming to f3, whereupon the h4-pawn falls.

33...♗xe2 34 ♔xe2 ♔f7 35 ♘f3 ♔g6 36 ♘xh4+

Now it's all over and Nigel makes a neat job of the technical phase of the game.

36...♔h5 37 ♘f3 ♘e7 38 ♘g5 ♘g6 39 ♘xe6 ♘h4 40 ♘c7 ♘xg2 41 ♘xd5 ♘h4 42 ♘f6+ ♔g6 43 d5 ♔f7 44 ♘h5 g2 45 ♔f2 ♔e7 46 ♘g3 ♔d7 47 ♘e2 b5 48 ♔g3 ♘g6 49 ♔xg2 a5 50 ♔g3 ♘e7 51 ♘d4 ♘xd5 52 ♘xf5 ♘c3 53 a3 ♘b1 54 h4 ♘xa3 55 h5 a4 56 bxa4 b4 57 ♘d4 ♘c4 58 ♘b3 ♔e6 59 ♔g4 ♘e3+ 60 ♔g5 ♔d5 61 h6 ♔c4 62 ♘a5+ 1-0

Key Points

1. Chess books can be immensely helpful if they are read in the right way. Look for inspiring ideas to improve your game, rather than typos or author oversights.

2. The books that are most highly thought of are not necessarily the most useful. Go with those that you find to be readable; a book will not help you at all if it is just sitting on the shelf.

3. Use a board and pieces rather than trying to skim read. Ideally the reader should use the book as a springboard for his own analysis.

4. Rereading can be very useful. With some of the best books there are new lessons to be learned as your appreciation of the authors' ideas becomes deeper.

Chapter Eight

Select your Chess Events Wisely

One aspect of the improvement process players rarely look at is the issue of event selection. For players at club level this might not seem something over which they have much control, as it can be hard enough to negotiate any time for chess at all. Nevertheless, there are always a few options and that is what I will discuss in this chapter.

For many people with little time for chess the default option is internet blitz, in which the players have five minutes or less for the entire game. I cannot warn too strongly against taking this route if you want to improve, the problem being that playing too many games at a fast time limit will corrupt the decision making process. Instead of playing good moves, a player honed on blitz will look for moves he can make quickly and perhaps bring himself closer to a win on time. Needless to say, this is not a good way to play 'real' chess, and the habits

acquired at faster time limits do spill over.

The very best training for 'real', terrestrial, tournament chess are games played at the same time limit. To maintain good form this should mean, ideally, around 50-70 'real' tournament games played face to face with a living opponent. Of course this is not possible for everybody; many players will struggle to get in even 10 or 20 games. So what should they do?

The answer is to supplement real games with a mix of online correspondence and live internet chess played at a slower time limit, looking to spend an equivalent number of man hours playing chess, but with the benefits of greater flexibility. As a rough guide you should look to spend three to four hours on each correspondence game that you play, and then have some sessions of live internet games of at least an hour's duration. A good ball park figure to aim for is at least 150 hours play per annum.

What are the most suitable time limits? It depends on the strength of the player; essentially you need to keep to time limits in which the chess position is more relevant than the thinking time and, ideally, much more relevant. I actually believe that only Grandmasters (2500+) should play five minute blitz, and that you should add another minute for every 50 points below 2500. Accordingly, 1500 players should have at least 25 minutes thinking time for a game – or a rough equivalent if they are using an incremental time limits.

As an example of a decent mix, let's say that John Doe, rated 1750, can only play 11 league games per annum, plus a single rapidplay event (30 minutes per game). This is way too little to maintain decent form, so in John Doe's case he might try to play 25 correspondence games per annum, and then have an hour per week playing a live internet game. This will take him up to around the requisite yearly figure of 150 hours.

Game Selection and Tiredness

There is a second major issue with tournament selection and that is to try and avoid playing when you are tired. Besides directly worsening your play, it can also have a more insidious effect of developing a 'tired style'. What I mean is that a player can get used to not put-

ting his best efforts into a game, and especially not calculating when it is needed. After a while this can become the way that someone plays even when they're as fresh as a daisy.

The following case history is a wonderful example of this effect and how it can lead to a dramatic improvement in results, if and when it is addressed.

Case History: Ken Alexander

When Ken consulted me it was apparent that he played far less well in the games after work than in weekend tournaments. There was also an issue with his openings in that they did not produce the kind of clear and logical play in which he excelled. After an overhaul of his repertoire, a switch to endgame orientated play, and abandoning evening games, his chess improved hugely. If fact he won his very next tournament.

The first game is a tired effort from before he made the changes; the second and third are from a weekend event afterwards. The difference in his play is quite amazing and demonstrates what a powerful improvement method tournament selection can be.

Game 47
K.Alexander-I.Annetts
Club Match, England 2007
Sicilian Defence

1 e4 c5 2 ♘c3 ♘c6 3 g3 ♘f6 4 ♗g2 g6 5

d3 ♗g7 6 ♗e3 d6 7 h3 a6

Too slow; it doesn't even 'threaten' ...b7-b5 because of e4-e5. Black should play 7...0-0, when 8 ♕d2 ♘d4 9 ♘ce2 e5 10 c3 ♘c6 11 f4 b6?! (11...♖e8 seems better) 12 ♘f3 exf4 13 ♗xf4 ♗a6 14 0-0 ♖e8 15 c4 b5 16 cxb5 ♗xb5 17 ♖f2 gave both sides chances in L.Ljubojevic-J.Sunye Neto, Brasilia 1981.

8 ♕d2 ♖b8 9 ♗h6 0-0 10 ♗xg7 ♔xg7 11 f4 b5?

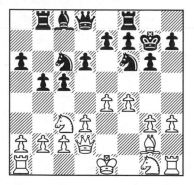

Losing a piece, and what should be the game. Black's best plan might be to put some pawns on dark squares. For example, 11...e5 12 ♘ge2 ♕e7 13 0-0-0 ♘d4 14 g4 was played in Ngo Thi Cam-Le Thanh Huyen, Vietnamese Team Championship 2002, and now 14...♘xe2+ 15 ♘xe2 exf4 16 ♕xf4 ♕e5 doesn't look too bad.

12 e5! ♘h5 13 ♗xc6 ♘xg3 14 ♖h2 dxe5 15 fxe5

When the opponent is down it's good to try and stick the boot in before he cobbles together some more resistance. To that end 15 ♕e3! would have been much stronger, the point being

that 15...exf4 16 ♕e5+ wins the b8-rook.

15...♕c7 16 ♕g5 ♘f5

Now Black is getting another pawn for the piece, plus some play. So White needs to be careful.

17 ♗h1?

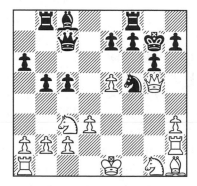

Another dodgy move, after which Black is right back in it. 17 ♗e4 b4 18 ♘d1 ♕xe5 19 ♘f3 looks like a better way for White.

17...♕xe5+

17...b4 is interesting. With only two pawns for the piece Black shouldn't have enough, but it's not easy.

18 ♖e2 ♕g3+ 19 ♕xg3 ♘xg3 20 ♖h2 e5 21 ♗f3 f5

After White's reply Black's pawn structure gets compromised. He should have tried something else; 21...f6, for example.

22 ♔f2 f4 23 ♘ge2

23 ♖e1!? looks stronger, as 23...♖e8 24 ♗c6 ♖e6 25 ♗d5 ♖e8 26 ♘f3 ♔f6 27 ♗c6 ♖e6 28 ♘e4+ ♘xe4+ 29 ♗xe4 nicely blockades Black's pawns.

23...♘f5 24 ♘d1?!

Too passive; 24 ♘e4 is much better.

24...♗e6 25 a4 b4 26 b3 g5 27 ♗g4 ♔f6 28 ♗xf5 ♔xf5

White's pieces have found themselves on passive squares, and this last exchange is an ominous sign. The knights aren't going to be much good at blockading Black's passed pawns.

29 ♘b2 h5 30 ♖g1 ♖g8 31 ♘c4 ♗xc4 32 dxc4

32 bxc4 was better, though 32...b3 would still be good for Black.

32...♖bd8

Now Black effectively has three pawns for the piece since White's queenside majority is immobile.

33 ♔e1 e4 34 ♖f2 ♔e5

35 ♘c1?

35 h4 was mandatory, trying to break up Black's pawn mass.

35...f3 36 ♖d2?!

Hastening the end.

36...♖xd2 37 ♔xd2 ♔f4 38 ♘e2+ fxe2 39 ♔xe2 g4 40 hxg4 hxg4 41 ♖f1+ ♔e5 0-1

Game 48
J.Clark-K.Alexander
Bideford 2008
Colle System

1 d4 d5 2 e3

The Colle is a popular opening at club level because it's easy to remember. The drawback is that it's rather predictable and a cunning opponent can adapt his formation to meet it.

2...♘f6 3 ♘f3 ♗g4

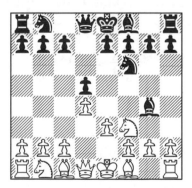

4 ♘bd2

White's most challenging move is 4 c4, after which 4...c6 would transpose into a Slav Defence. The passive text presents Black with at least equality.

4...e6 5 ♗e2 ♗d6 6 0-0 0-0 7 h3 ♗h5 8 c4 c5

Another good move is 8...c6.

9 dxc5 ♗xc5 10 ♖e1

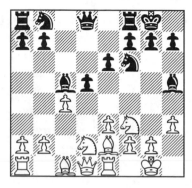

10 a3 would have been better, intending b2-b4 and ♗c1-b2. The text is a typical move in the Colle System, but it's not very relevant in this particular position.

10...♘c6 11 cxd5 ♘xd5

11...exd5 was not bad either, although the dynamic nature of isolated d-pawn positions does not suit everyone.

12 ♘b3 ♗b6 13 a3 ♕f6 14 g4?!

Stuck for a plan White lashes out, making his position much worse. However, it's not easy to find a move for White here; for example, seeking exchanges via 14 ♘fd2 still leaves him stuck following 14...♗g6 and 15...♖fd8.

14...♗g6 15 ♔g2?!

After Black's reply White does not have a good move, so probably he should try something else here. 15 ♘bd4 looks like the best, though it is hardly promising for White after just

15...♖ac8.

15...♖fd8 16 ♘bd4 ♖ac8 17 g5 ♕e7

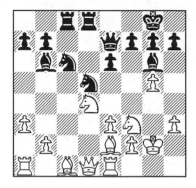

18 ♕a4?!

White is probably losing in any case but now his position rapidly falls apart. He should exchange on c6 before playing 19 ♕a4.

18...♘xd4 19 exd4 ♗c2 20 b3 ♘c3

Winning material; but 20...♗e4! would have been even stronger.

21 ♕b4 ♕xb4 22 axb4 ♗xb3 23 ♖a3?!

23 ♗e3 was relatively best, though Black is still winning after 23...♘xe2 24 ♖xe2 ♗d5 etc.

23...♘xe2 24 ♖xe2 ♗d1

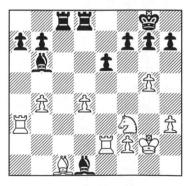

Winning a piece. White could have

saved himself the rest, but he fights on gamely to the end.

25 ♖e1 ♖xc1 26 ♔f1 ♖dc8 27 ♖xd1 ♖xd1+ 28 ♔e2 ♖dc1 29 ♖d3 ♖1c4 30 d5 ♖c2+ 31 ♘d2 exd5 32 ♖xd5 ♖d8 33 ♖xd8+ ♗xd8 34 ♔d3 ♖xd2+ 35 ♔xd2 ♗xg5+ 36 ♔c3 ♔f8 37 ♔c4 ♔e8 38 ♔d5 ♔d7 39 f3 ♗e7 40 b5 a6 41 bxa6 bxa6 42 ♔c4 a5 43 ♔b5 ♗d8 0-1

> ## Game 49
> ## K.Alexander-A.Fraser
> Braintree 2008
> *London System*

1 d4 ♘f6 2 ♗f4

The London System was also part of our grand plan, though I try to encourage the development of knights before bishops; i.e. playing 2 ♘f3 first.

2...e6 3 e3 d5 4 ♘f3

White can also safeguard his bishop from exchange with 4 h3.

4...♘h5

5 ♗g3

Alternatively White could have played 5 ♗g5, when 5...♗e7 (and not 5...f6 6 ♗h4 g5 because of 7 ♘xg5) 6 ♗xe7 ♕xe7 7 ♘bd2 might offer him a tiny plus.

5...♗b4+?!

Giving check can sometimes make people feel good about themselves, but this gives White a free move. Exchanging the dark-squared bishop with 5...♘xg3 was a better idea, after which 6 hxg3 g6 and 7...♗g7 would help solidify Black's kingside.

6 c3 ♘xg3 7 hxg3 ♗e7 8 ♘bd2 ♘d7 9 ♗d3 g6 10 c4 c5?!

This leaves Black saddled with an isolated d-pawn. 10...c6 would have been far more solid.

11 cxd5 exd5 12 dxc5 ♘xc5 13 ♗b5+ ♗d7 14 ♗xd7+ ♘xd7

And here 14...♕xd7 is better, with Black having a perfectly playable position after 15 0-0 0-0 16 ♘b3 ♘e6.

15 0-0 0-0 16 ♘b3 ♘b6

Again not the best. 16...♘f6 was preferable, with ideas of coming into e4.

17 ♘bd4 ♗f6 18 b3 ♘c8 19 ♖c1 ♘e7 20

♖c2 ♕d7 21 ♕d2 ♖fc8 22 ♖fc1 ♘f5?

Losing the d5-pawn. Black should have played 22...♖xc2 23 ♖xc2 ♖c8, when White has a slight edge but no more than that.

23 ♘xf5 ♕xf5

Now on 23...♖xc2 White has 24 ♘h6+ (24 ♕xc2 ♕xf5 25 ♕c7 b6 26 g4!? is also good, since 26...♕xg4 27 ♕c6 forks c8 and f6) 24...♔g7 25 ♕xc2 ♔xh6 26 ♕c7 ♖d8 27 ♕f4+ ♔g7 28 ♖c7, winning a pawn.

24 ♖xc8+ ♖xc8 25 ♖xc8+ ♕xc8

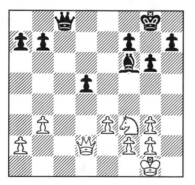

26 ♕xd5

Picking up a pawn while leaving White with queen and knight vs. queen and bishop. This is thought to be an advantage because these pieces cooperate well together.

26...♕c1+ 27 ♔h2 ♕b2 28 ♕d2 ♕a3 29 ♕c2 b6 30 ♘d2 h5 31 ♘e4 ♗b2 32 ♕b1 ♗e5 33 f4

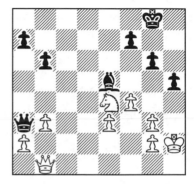

A good plan. By advancing on the kingside White will be able to inflict weaknesses on Black's king position, and then hopefully exploit this with his queen and knight combo.

33...♗b2 34 ♘g5 ♗f6 35 ♘f3

White's e-pawn is now ready to roll forward.

35...♕e7 36 e4 g5?!

A bad move which leaves White with a winning position. 36...♕d7 was a better way of trying to keep him at bay.

37 e5 ♗g7 38 ♘xg5

This win of a second pawn spells the beginning of the end for Black.

38...f6 39 exf6 ♗xf6 40 ♕g6+ ♕g7 41 ♕xg7+

Good enough.

41...♔xg7 42 ♘e4 ♗e7 43 ♔h3 ♔g6 44 g4 hxg4+ 45 ♔xg4 b5 46 f5+ ♔g7

47 f6+

The king and pawn endgame is easily won for White.

47...♗xf6 48 ♘xf6 ♔xf6 49 ♔f4 a5 50 ♔e4 ♔e6 51 ♔d4 ♔d6 52 a4 bxa4 53 bxa4 ♔c6 54 ♔c4 ♔b6 55 ♔d5 ♔c7 56 ♔c5 1-0

Key Points

1. To maintain good form you need at least 150 hours serious playing time per annum.

2. If you cannot play enough competitive over-the-board games, supplement those which you can play with a mixture of correspondence chess and online games played at slower time limits (e.g. 30 minutes per player per game).

3. The lower your rating, the more thinking time you need in order to develop good chess habits.

4. Try to avoid playing when you are tired, because this can lead to poor thinking traits that spill over into all your games.

Chapter Nine

Know your Enemy

"Know your enemy as you know yourself and you can fight a hundred battles with no danger of defeat." – Sun Tzu (*The Art of War*)

"You can discover what your enemy fears most by observing the means he uses to frighten you." – Eric Hoffer (*The Passionate State of Mind*)

Over my years of playing and teaching chess I have often been struck by how fanciful our ideas can be about what is required for combat. This is particularly noticeable with regard to the opening, and I sometimes see people who have barely learned how the pieces move wanting to play openings used by world champions.

Other players have the idea that they need to memorize twenty moves of theory in order to conduct the opening stage reasonably well. They do not stop to consider whether their opponents will have enough knowledge to cooperate, or what they will do when these twenty moves are over. This belief does them a massive disservice, in that they can waste a huge amount of time studying openings material they can never use. It also distracts their attention from other more important aspects of the game.

Accordingly we should try to gain insight into the two main enemies we have on the chessboard, our opponents and ourselves.

One of the most useful habits I developed for chess was to write down the thoughts I had during the game on the scoresheet. Some of this would be done during post mortem analysis, but I would also write my own more private notes after returning to my room. Basically these private notes would detail any concerns I had during the game; for example, if I was uncomfortable in the opening and felt I needed to study a particular line.

The point of making such notes at this particular time was that it was a way of 'keeping it real'. I know that I get all sorts of wonderful ideas about what I need to do with my chess once I am away from the tournament hall; for example, it sometimes occurs to me that I should play open Sicilians as White! Once or twice I have tried to act on these more unrealistic notions: at one time I spent a number of weeks trying to learn the Botvinnik Variation of the Semi-Slav as White. The first game in which I actually played this was an unmitigated disaster.

Occasionally I have kept a tournament diary, detailing my thoughts and feelings before each game, doing the same thing afterwards and making notes to the game. I gained a great deal of insight by doing this, though to some extent it interfered with my prime directive to relax during chess events. These days I only use the scoresheet.

Observational practices such as these can help considerably with understanding how we really think during games, and I have also learned a lot about player psychology through my extensive teaching practice. It's a very far cry from most people's beliefs.

Let's now take a look at two specific aspects of chess player psychology in which a knowledge of our enemies

(ourselves and our opponents) is of great value. The first is that of playing for a draw and the emotions this involves, and the second is that of Pavlovian responses.

Playing for a draw

Playing directly for a draw is known to be a mistaken strategy because you thereby put yourself in a defensive and negative frame of mind. The right way to do it is to play well during a game and then offer a draw from a position of strength. It is very unlikely that it will be declined.

If, on the other hand, your position is not that strong, a draw offer can be seen as a sign of weakness and even encourage the other player to chance his arm. Generally speaking one should only offer a draw to those who have an incentive of some sort to accept.

Prior to the following game Efim Geller had an excellent personal score against Bobby Fischer. As he also had White he was probably expecting his draw offer to be accepted without a second thought. When Fischer refused, Geller was clearly shaken...

Game 50
E.Geller-R.J.Fischer
Palma de Mallorca
Interzonal 1970
Grünfeld Defence

1 ♘f3 ♘f6 2 c4 g6 3 g3 ♗g7 4 ♗g2 0-0

5 0-0 c6 6 d4 d5 7 cxd5

With this move Geller offered a draw – which was greeted by laughter from Fischer. As Geller was leading 5-2 in wins (with two draws) before this game, this showed remarkable self confidence on Fischer's part.

7...cxd5 8 ♘e5 ♗f5 9 ♘c3 ♘e4

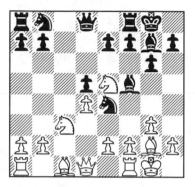

10 ♗e3

10 ♘xe4 is better, though this does not look great for White either; for example, 10...♗xe4 11 ♗f4 ♗xg2 12 ♔xg2 ♕b6 13 ♕d2 ♗xe5 14 ♗xe5 ♘c6 is fine for Black.

10...♘xc3 11 bxc3 ♘c6 12 ♘xc6 bxc6 13 ♕a4 ♕b6 14 ♖ac1 ♖ab8 15 c4 ♗xd4 16 ♗xd4 ♕xd4 17 e3?

After this Black has the advantage. White should have played 17 ♖fd1, when 17...♕b2 18 cxd5 cxd5 19 ♗xd5 ♕xe2 20 ♕xa7 would probably be a draw.

17...♕e5 18 cxd5 cxd5 19 ♖fd1 e6 20 ♕xa7 ♖a8 21 ♕d4 ♕xd4 22 ♖xd4 ♖xa2 23 e4 dxe4 24 ♗xe4 ♗xe4 25 ♖xe4

With best play this endgame should still be a draw, but with an extra pawn Black clearly has whatever chances are going.

25...♖b8 26 ♖e3 g5

A typical and thematic move. Black gains space while making it difficult for White to advance his kingside pawns (f2-f4 or h2-h4) without getting them split.

27 h3 ♔g7 28 ♖c7 ♔g6 29 ♖f3 f6 30 ♖e7 ♖e2 31 g4 ♖b1+ 32 ♔g2 ♖ee1 33 ♖a3 h5 34 ♖aa7 ♖g1+ 35 ♔f3 hxg4+ 36 hxg4 ♖b3+ 37 ♔e2 ♖xg4 38 ♖xe6

This further exchange of pawns brings the draw that little bit closer. But White still has to play accurately.

38...♖b1 39 ♖aa6 ♖f4 40 ♖a2 ♖h1 41

♖ea6 ♖b4 42 ♖6a4 ♖bb1 43 ♖a8 ♖hg1 44 ♔f3 ♖b5 45 ♖8a5 ♖b3+ 46 ♔e2 ♖bb1 47 ♖a8 ♔f5 48 ♖2a5+ ♔g4 49 ♖a4+ ♔h5 50 ♖h8+ ♔g6 51 ♖g8+ ♔f7 52 ♖d8 ♖be1+ 53 ♔f3 ♖e5 54 ♖d2 ♖f5+ 55 ♔e2 ♖e5+ 56 ♔f3 ♔g6

This position was reached after the second time control. White should be able to draw, but in practice he still needs to be careful.

57 ♖e4 ♖f5+ 58 ♔e2 ♖a5 59 ♖e3 ♔h5 60 ♖ed3 ♖aa1 61 ♖d8 f5 62 ♔f3 ♖a3+ 63 ♖2d3 g4+ 64 ♔f4 ♖xd3 65 ♖xd3 ♖f1 66 ♖d2?

It seems that the Soviet contingent were horrified when they saw this move. They had analysed 66 ♔g3, which should lead to a draw.

66...♔h4 67 ♔xf5 g3

Geller had thought this move impossible, and was intending to answer it by taking on g3 with check, followed by taking the rook on f1 with his king. After seven hours of torture, the mind can play tricks.

68 f4 ♔h3 69 ♖d3 ♔h4 70 ♖d2 ♖a1 71 ♔e5 ♔g4 72 f5 ♖a5+ 73 ♔d4 ♖xf5 0-1

The following game is an object lesson in the art of playing for a win, and especially in exploiting the nervousness of a player who needs a draw. At this point in the match Karpov was leading 12-11, so a draw would see him regain his title. Kasparov, on the other hand, *had* to win.

So what does he do? Not very much in fact, except to put his opponent in a long drawn out struggle. The idea is that in a long game the jitters will have plenty of opportunity to show themselves.

> *Game 51*
> **G.Kasparov-A.Karpov**
> World Championship (24th matchgame), Seville 1987
> *English Opening*

1 c4 e6 2 ♘f3 ♘f6 3 g3 d5 4 b3 ♗e7 5 ♗g2 0-0 6 0-0 b6 7 ♗b2 ♗b7 8 e3 ♘bd7

Karpov's scheme varies from my game against Thorhallsson (Game 22) in that he does not play the advance ...c7-c5. This leaves Black with fewer strategic responsibilities, but also less space.

9 ♘c3 ♘e4 10 ♘e2!?

Kasparov, in turn, keeps as much tension in the position as he can by avoiding simplification. Not that it is bad to exchange pieces when playing for a win; it just keeps maximum pressure on the opponent who needs a draw.

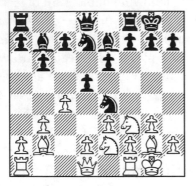

10...a5 11 d3 ♗f6 12 ♕c2 ♗xb2 13 ♕xb2 ♘d6 14 cxd5 ♗xd5

Black could also play 14...exd5!?, after which 15 d4 c5 16 dxc5 bxc5 would lead to an unclear 'hanging pawn' position. However, Karpov was hardly likely to choose such a tense line given the match situation.

15 d4! c5 16 ♖fd1 ♖c8?!

Already preparing the exchange he makes on his next move, which requires moving the rook from a8. But perhaps Black should have played 16...♕e7 intending 17 ♘f4 ♗e4.

17 ♘f4 ♗xf3 18 ♗xf3 ♕e7 19 ♖ac1 ♖fd8 20 dxc5 ♘xc5 21 b4!

Taking the initiative by targeting the pawn on b6. The position is now reminiscent of a Catalan, with White having a small but nagging advantage.

21...axb4 22 ♕xb4 ♕a7 23 a3 ♘f5 24 ♖b1 ♖xd1+ 25 ♖xd1 ♕c7 26 ♘d3! h6?!

Under immense psychological pressure Karpov starts making some small inaccuracies. 26...g6! would have been better, making room for Black's king on the opposite colour squares to White's remaining bishop.

27 ♖c1 ♘e7?!

At first sight 27...♘xd3? 28 ♖xc7 ♖xc7 looks tempting, but it does not work because of 29 ♕e4 ♖c1+ 30 ♔g2 ♘e1+ 31 ♔h3 etc. However, Black could have played more accurately here with 27...♘d6, preventing 28 ♕b5.

28 ♕b5 ♘f5 29 a4 ♘d6 30 ♕b1 ♕a7 31 ♘e5! ♘xa4?

Karpov tries to simplify the position, but in doing so makes a serious error. He should have played 31...♕xa4 32 ♕xb6 ♕a3!, when it would be difficult for White to prove anything.

32 ♖xc8+ ♘xc8

33 ♕d1??

The clock was playing its part here. Kasparov should have played 33 ♕b5!, when 33...♔h7 (33...♘d6 is strongly met by 34 ♕c6) 34 ♕e8 ♘d6 35 ♕d8 ♘f5 (after 35...♘b7 White plays 36 ♕f8!) 36 ♘c6 ♕b7 37 g4 wins a piece.

33...♘e7??

A serious mistake which allows White to win the f7-pawn. 33...♘c5! would have left the position equal and probably allowed Karpov to regain the world title.

34 ♕d8+ ♔h7 35 ♘xf7 ♘g6 36 ♕e8 ♕e7 37 ♕xa4 ♕xf7 38 ♗e4

Although the pawns are restricted to one side of the board, this position is highly unpleasant for Black. Whether he is objectively lost is almost immaterial, what matters is that the practical difficulties are so great that the odds are heavily stacked in White's favour.

38...♔g8 39 ♕b5 ♘f8 40 ♕xb6 ♕f6 41 ♕b5 ♕e7 42 ♔g2 g6 43 ♕a5 ♕g7 44 ♕c5 ♕f7 45 h4 h5?

Apparently the decisive mistake, and it's interesting that this should

come during the adjournment. 45...♔g7 was much better, simply waiting.

46 ♕c6 ♕e7 47 ♗d3 ♕f7 48 ♕d6 ♔g7 49 e4 ♔g8 50 ♗c4 ♔g7 51 ♕e5+ ♔g8 52 ♕d6 ♔g7 53 ♗b5 ♔g8 54 ♗c6 ♕a7 55 ♕b4! ♕c7 56 ♕b7! ♕d8

Black cannot afford to exchange queens now, as after 56...♕xb7 57 ♗xb7 ♘d7 58 f4 his position would be slowly infiltrated by White's king and bishop.

57 e5! ♕a5 58 ♗e8 ♕c5 59 ♕f7+ ♔h8 60 ♗a4 ♕d5+ 61 ♔h2 ♕c5

On 61...♘h7 there follows 62 ♗c2 ♕xe5 63 ♕e8+ etc.

62 ♗b3 ♕c8 63 ♗d1 ♕c5 64 ♔g2 1-0

After 64...♕b4 65 ♗f3 ♕c5 66 ♗e4 ♕b4 67 f3! (but not 67 ♗xg6? because of 67...♘xg6 68 ♕xg6 ♕b7+ 69 ♔g1 ♕h1+! forcing stalemate) 67...♕d2+ 68 ♔h3 ♕b4 69 ♗xg6 ♘xg6 70 ♕xg6 ♕xh4+ 71 ♔g2!, White avoids stalemate and wins.

This next game shows a different slant on the offer of a draw, in that I used it to deliberately annoy an opponent and lower his vigilance. There was a deep and cunning trap in the position which was more likely to catch an angry opponent.

Game 52
N.Davies-D.Kaiumov
Calcutta 1997
English Opening

---

1 c4 ♘f6 2 ♘f3 b6 3 g3 c5 4 ♗g2 ♗b7 5 0-0 e6 6 ♘c3 a6 7 ♖e1

One of my favourite lines, which has more than a few traps.

7...♗e7 8 e4 d6 9 d4 cxd4 10 ♘xd4 ♕c7

One of the points behind this line is that the natural-looking 10...♘bd7 runs into 11 e5! dxe5 12 ♗xb7 exd4 13 ♗xa8 and White wins the exchange for inadequate compensation. I've managed to pull that one off several times in weekend tournaments.

11 ♗e3 ♘bd7 12 ♖c1 0-0 13 f4 ♖fd8 14 f5

14...♘f8

Black has also tried 14...e5, but then 15 ♘d5 is good for White; for example, 15...♗xd5? (15...♘xd5 16 cxd5 ♘c5 is a better bet, though White is still for choice after 17 ♘f3 a5 18 ♘d2) 16 cxd5 ♕b7 17 ♘c6 ♖e8 18 g4 and White's position was overwhelming in L.Psakhis-K.Hovmoller, Copenhagen 2000.

15 ♕e2

In the cold light of day it seems quite promising to play 15 fxe6 fxe6 16 ♗h3, when 16...♗c8 (not 16...♘xe4? 17 ♘xe6) 17 ♖f1 leaves Black rather tied up.

15...♖e8 16 g4 h6 17 h4

In retrospect these pawn advances were probably hurting me more than my opponent, but a degree of machismo was creeping in at this point.

17...♘6h7 18 ♕f2 ♗f6 19 ♘f3 ♘d7 20 fxe6 fxe6 21 g5 hxg5 22 hxg5 ♗e5 23 ♕h4

It was around here that I made my first draw offer, hoping that my inferior position would be disguised by some aggressive-looking pieces. But my opponent refused.

23...♘hf8 24 ♕g4 g6 25 ♖ed1 ♗g7 26 ♗f4 ♕c5+ 27 ♔h2 ♘e5 28 ♘xe5 ♗xe5 29 ♗xe5 dxe5

This position is just good for Black, the doubled e-pawns being more than compensated for by his control of terrain and key squares.

30 ♘e2 ♖ad8 31 b3 a5 32 ♘g1 ♖d4 33 ♘e2 ♖d6 34 ♖xd6 ♕xd6 35 ♘g1 ♖d8 36 ♘f3 ♖d7 37 ♖e1 ♖h7+ 38 ♔g1 a4 39 ♕g3 ♘d7 40 ♘h2 ♖f7 41 ♘g4 ♖f4 42 ♘f2 axb3 43 axb3 ♗c6

At this point I spotted a really cunning trap, but would the guy fall for it? Maybe not unless I raised his blood pressure a little, so after my next move I threw in an insulting draw offer. This was particularly poor etiquette on my part because I had already offered one earlier in the game.

44 ♘d3 ♕d4+ 45 ♕e3 ♖g4 46 ♔h2 ♕xe3 47 ♖xe3 ♖xg5?

Hook line and sinker!! White's next move traps his rook on g5.

48 ♗f3 ♘f6 49 ♘f2

Threatening 50 ♘h3, not to men-

tion an advance of the queenside pawns. Black tries to fight on by giving up a piece.

49...♘h5 50 ♖e1 ♖g3 51 ♗xh5 ♖xb3 52 ♖g1 ♔f8 53 ♖xg6 ♔e7 54 ♗g4 ♗d7 55 ♘h3 ♖c3 56 ♘g5 ♖xc4 57 ♗xe6 ♖c2+ 58 ♔g3 ♗e8 59 ♖h6 ♖c1 60 ♗g4 ♖g1+ 61 ♔f3 ♗a4 62 ♖e6+ ♔f8 63 ♘h7+ ♔f7 64 ♗f5 b5 65 ♖b6 ♔g7 66 ♖b7+ ♔h6 67 ♘f6 ♖f1+ 68 ♔g2 ♖b1 69 ♘d5 ♗d1 70 ♘c3 ♖b2+ 71 ♔g3 ♖b3 72 ♔h4! 1-0

Mate on h7 is coming.

Pavlovian Responses

The field of Pavlovian responses in chess is one that I believe I have pioneered. It is a sensitive subject for many chess players, because they do not like the idea that they can behave like the hounds conditioned in Ivan Pavlov's experiments. Nevertheless, I have noticed that there are areas in which conditioned reflexes take over, which offer a variety of applications for the cunning and enterprising player.

The simplest and most direct use is in opening selection. At club level I have noticed that the fianchetto of a king's bishop is often met by an attempt to exchange it, regardless of whether or not this is a good idea. This was probably conditioned into many club players by seeing games with the Sicilian Dragon and White's attempt to give mate in the Yugoslav Attack (1 e4 c5 2 ♘f3 d6 3 d4 cxd4 4 ♘xd4 ♘f6 5 ♘c3 g6 6 ♗e3 ♗g7 7 f3 ♘c6 8 ♕d2 0-0 9 0-0-0 with ideas of ♗e3-h6 and h2-h4-h5). Yet, in very many instances it is quite inappropriate, such as in some lines of the Pirc Defence...

> ## Game 53
> **F.Cavalcanti-C.E.Toth**
> Brazilian Championship,
> Porto Alegre 1990
> *Modern Defence*

1 e4 d6 2 d4 ♘f6 3 ♘c3 g6 4 ♗e3 c6

This is another way to try and exploit White's ♗h6 anti-fianchetto plan: Black doesn't even waste time by moving his bishop to g7. Interestingly White seems oblivious to both this and Black's right to castle on the queenside; he just proceeds blindly with his plan of attack.

5 ♕d2 b5 6 f3 ♗g7

There's a case for delaying this further and playing 6...♘bd7, when 7 ♗h6 would lose a tempo compared with the game.

7 ♗h6 ♗xh6 8 ♕xh6 ♘bd7 9 g4 ♕b6 10 0-0-0 ♗b7 11 ♘h3 0-0-0

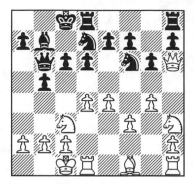

12 ♗e2

This 'developing move' makes little sense in this specific position because the knight on c3 would like the option to go back there. 12 ♔b1 is better.

12...b4 13 ♘a4 ♕a5 14 b3 ♘b6 15 ♘xb6+ axb6 16 ♔b1 ♔c7 17 ♕c1 ♖a8 18 ♕b2 ♖a7

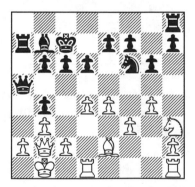

19 e5??

Continuing with the kingside attacking moves to the end, but this one loses on the spot. Driving the knight to d5 would be a good idea with Black's king on g8 and White's queen on h6; here it is just suicidal.

19...♘d5 0-1

Black's threat to come into c3 causes mayhem.

An even better way to exploit the Pavlovian response to fianchettos is to play the Accelerated Dragon. Looking almost exactly like a Dragon it should, at club level, elicit the usual response of ♗e3 and ♕d2 etc. But there is a very important difference in that Black has not spent a tempo on ...d7-d6.

Game 54
M.Hughes-N.Davies
North Wales 1983
Sicilian Defence

---

1 e4 c5 2 ♘f3 ♘c6

Later on I started experimenting with the provocative 2...g6 in order to throw my opponents on their own resources. Unfortunately this also had the effect of throwing me on my own resources, and I tended to do worse than in a standard Accelerated Dragon.
3 d4 cxd4 4 ♘xd4 g6 5 ♗e3

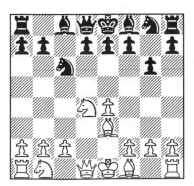

Already salivating at the thought of exchanging my dark-squared bishop with ♕d1-d2 and ♗e3-h6 and then mating me down the h-file. At GM level White's most popular option is the Maróczy Bind with 5 c4, but this requires quite sophisticated positional understanding to play well. What I've noticed is that even if club players are aware of this line they tend to play it badly for White, either exchanging dark-squared bishops or lashing out with f2-f4.
5...♘f6 6 ♘c3 ♗g7 7 ♕d2 0-0 8 f3

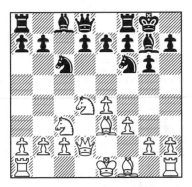

Exactly the same formula as the one White uses in a 2...d6 Dragon, but Black's next move shows the difference.
8...d5!

The point – compared to a regular Dragon with 9 0-0-0 (1 e4 c5 2 ♘f3 d6 3 d4 cxd4 4 ♘xd4 ♘f6 5 ♘c3 g6 6 ♗e3 ♗g7 7 ♕d2 0-0 8 f3 ♘c6 9 0-0-0 d5!?), Black is a clear tempo ahead. This is by virtue of having moved his d-pawn to d5 in one go instead of two.
9 ♘xc6 bxc6 10 exd5 ♘xd5 11 ♗d4

White is still playing all the same

moves that he would use in the 2...d6 and 9 0-0-0 line. Needless to say the lost tempo will make a big difference.

11...e5 12 ♗c5 ♖e8 13 ♘e4 ♖b8 14 c3 f5!

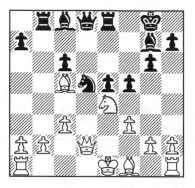

15 ♘d6

Losing material, but the alternatives are not much better. After 15 ♘f2 Black can play 15...e4!, when 16 fxe4 ♖xb2 17 ♕xb2 ♗xc3+ wins the white queen.

15...♗f8 16 c4

16 ♘xe8 ♗xc5 wins the knight on e8. If White tries to rescue it with 17 c4 then 17...♗b4 wins his queen.

16...♗xd6 17 ♗xd6 ♕xd6 18 cxd5 cxd5 19 ♗e2 ♗e6 20 b3

Despite the loss of the pawn White is still unable to get his king safe. After 20 0-0 Black would win the b2-pawn with 20...♕b6+.

20...♕b6 21 h4

A last despairing throw.

21...♖bc8 22 h5 f4!

Stopping White's queen from going to h6.

23 hxg6 hxg6 24 ♔f1 ♔g7 25 g3 ♖h8 26 ♔g2

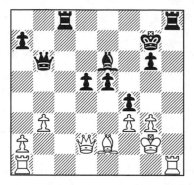

Allowing a nice finish, but there is little to be done in any case.

26...♗h3+ 27 ♖xh3 ♖xh3 28 ♕xd5

Or 28 ♔xh3 ♕f2 29 gxf4 ♖h8+ 30 ♔g4 ♕g2 mate.

28...♖xg3+ 0-1

It's mate next move.

I noticed another Pavlovian response in the Sicilian in that Black players will often try to play their favourite set-up regardless of the moves White comes out with – particularly in the 2 c3 variation: Black gets to play 2...d6, 3...cxd4 and 4...♘f6 just as he does in the open lines (2 ♘f3 and 3 d4), but the position he ends up with is very different.

Game 55
Smirin-S.Neff
Vilnius 1972
Sicilian Defence

1 e4 c5 2 c3 d6

This response is very common at

club level, by those who have learned the *moves* that lead to a Dragon or Najdorf, but apparently not noticed the fact that White has played 2 c3. This game illustrates exactly what I mean.

3 d4 cxd4

Black plays 3...cxd4 in the Sicilian, right? But in this case White has played 2 c3 followed by 3 d4 rather than 2 ♘f3 and 3 d4. Black's best move in this position is 3...♘f6, which is an interesting way to play it – assuming, of course, that Black knows what he's doing.

4 cxd4 ♘f6 5 ♘c3 e6

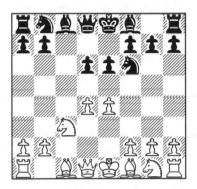

What usually happens here is that Black plays the move he uses in an open Sicilian, so I'd guess that Neff is a Scheveningen player (1 e4 c5 2 ♘f3 d6 3 d4 cxd4 4 ♘xd4 ♘f6 5 ♘c3 e6). Similarly a Dragon player would be likely to play 5...g6, while a Najdorf player would go 5...a6. In any case White has a nice position, having established his central pawns on d4 and e4 early on.

6 ♘f3 ♗e7 7 ♗d3 0-0

Given this position to play (and I would avoid it like the plague) I'd

probably close it up with 7...d5 8 e5 ♘fd7 and then keep my king in the centre for a while. Black's lagging development would be less likely to hurt him in this closed, French-like position.

8 0-0 a6 9 ♕e2

White's plan is not rocket science: he will play e4-e5 to drive the knight from f6 and then take pot-shots at Black's poorly defended king.

9...♘bd7 10 e5 ♘e8 11 ♘e4 d5 12 ♘eg5 g6 13 ♕e3 ♘g7 14 h4 f5

With the storm clouds gathering around his king Black tries to get some breathing space. Unfortunately for him, it's rather too late.

15 ♘h3 ♖e8 16 ♘fg5 ♘f8

After 16...♘b6, White wins with 17 ♘xh7! ♔xh7 18 ♕h6+ ♔g8 19 ♕xg6 ♗xh4 20 ♗g5.

17 g4! fxg4 18 ♕f4! gxh3?

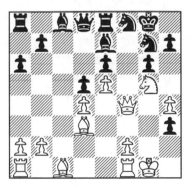

Losing. Black should play 18...♘f5, though he's still in serious trouble after 19 ♕xg4.

19 ♘f7 ♕c7

Allowing mate. 19...♗g5 20 hxg5 ♕e7 would have extended the game.

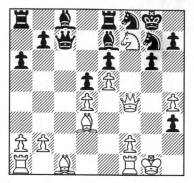

20 ♘h6+ ♔h8 21 ♕f7 1-0

Black is mated after 21...♘d7 22 ♕g8+ ♖xg8 23 ♘f7.

Case History: Femi Adebajo

Femi Adebajo was a psychiatrist and Sicilian Dragon enthusiast when he first consulted me. With a demanding schedule and many interests he found it difficult to find time for serious opening research, but I managed to persuade him that the *Accelerated Dragon* could exploit his opponents' Pavlovian responses. Although sceptical to begin with, he tried it and was amazed. At club level most players fail to see the important differences and allow Black to play ...d7-d5 in one move.

> ### Game 56
> **P.Fisher-F.Adebajo**
> Ebbw Vale 2009
> *Sicilian Defence*

1 e4 c5 2 ♘f3 g6 3 d4 cxd4 4 ♘xd4 ♗g7 5 ♗e3 ♘f6 6 ♘c3 0-0 7 ♗e2 ♘c6 8 0-0

If White wants to transpose into a 2...d6 Classical Dragon then the way to do it is via 8 ♘b3, preventing 8...d5. After the move played Black is already at least equal.

8...d5!

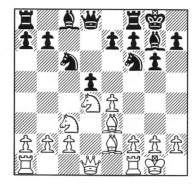

9 ♘xc6

On 9 exd5 ♘xd5 10 ♘xd5 ♕xd5 11 ♗f3 Black's best line appears to be 11...♕a5!, as demonstrated several times by Accelerated Dragon expert, John Donaldson. For example, 12 ♘xc6 (12 ♗xc6 bxc6 13 ♘xc6 ♕c7 14 ♘d4 ♗a6 15 ♖e1 ♖ad8 16 ♕g4 ♗c8 17 ♕e4 ♗b7 18 ♕g4 h5 19 ♘b5 ♕c6 20 ♕g5 f6 21 ♕xg6 ♕xb5 won a piece in D.Muller-J.Donaldson, Seattle 1980) 12...bxc6 13 c3 (13 ♗xc6 ♖b8 14 ♕d5 ♕c7 15 ♗a4 ♖xb2 16 ♕c5 ♕b7 17 ♗b3 ♗f5 was good for Black in G.Basanta-J.Donaldson, Seattle 1987) 13...♖b8 14 ♕c1 c5 15 ♖d1 ♗e6 was about equal at this point in A.La Vergue-J.Donaldson, Seattle 1987.

9...bxc6 10 e5 ♘d7

10...♘e4 is not bad, but against an opponent rated some 300 points lower than himself Black wishes to avoid any early simplification.

11 f4 e6 12 ♘a4 ♛a5?!

Both here and on the next move I would have undermined White's e5-pawn with ...f7-f6, thus bringing the Dragon bishop on g7 back to life.

13 b3 c5?! 14 ♗d2

14 ♛e1! seems to be White's best move here, when Black should play 14...♛c7 followed by 15...f6! to create counterplay.

14...♛c7 15 c3 ♗b7 16 ♗e3 ♖ac8 17 ♖c1 ♖fd8 18 ♛d2 ♛a5?!

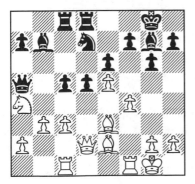

19 ♖fd1?!

Missing a tactic with 19 ♘xc5! ♘xc5

20 b4, after which 20...♘e4 21 bxa5 ♘xd2 22 ♗xd2 f6 23 exf6 ♗xf6 24 ♗e3 would keep an edge for White.

19...♗f8 20 ♛d3 c4!

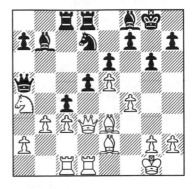

Seizing the initiative.

21 ♛d2 ♗c6 22 ♛c2

White should have tried 22 ♘b2, when 22...♛xa2 23 b4 ♛a6 24 ♖a1 would be very good for him. For Black, 22...♖b8 is better, meeting 23 b4 with 23...♛a3!.

22...♗xa4 23 bxa4 ♗c5 24 ♗d4 ♘b6

The a4-pawn is falling.

25 ♖f1 ♘xa4 26 ♗d1?

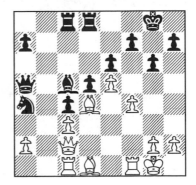

26...♘xc3!

This win of a second pawn is the

beginning of the end.

27 ♗xc5 ♕xc5+ 28 ♔h1 ♘xd1 29 ♖fxd1 ♖b8 30 ♕c3 ♖b6 31 ♖c2 ♖db8 32 h3 ♖b1 33 ♖dc1 ♖xc1+ 34 ♖xc1 ♕f2 35 ♕f3 ♕xf3 36 gxf3 ♖b2 37 a4 ♔g7 38 ♖c3 ♖b3 0-1

Game 57
O.Smith-F.Adebajo
British League 2009
Sicilian Defence

1 e4 c5 2 ♘f3 ♘c6 3 d4 cxd4 4 ♘xd4 g6 5 ♗e3 ♗g7 6 ♘c3 ♘f6 7 f3 0-0 8 ♗c4

White sees in the nick of time that Black can meet 8 ♕d2 with 8...d5!, but the text move also has its problems.
8...♕b6!

Suddenly setting up a variety of tactical threats, such as 9...♕xb2, 9...♘xe4 and 9...♘g4.
9 ♕d2

9 ♗b3 is White's best here, when 9...♘xe4 10 ♘d5 ♕a5+ 11 c3 ♘c5 12 ♘xc6 dxc6 13 ♘xe7+ ♔h8 14 ♘xc8 ♖axc8 15 0-0 produces stone cold

equality. 9...♘g4!? keeps more play in the position; for example, 10 fxg4 ♗xd4 11 ♗xd4 ♘xd4! 12 ♘d5 ♕a5+! 13 c3 ♘c6 gave both sides chances in B.Lugo-R.Hernandez Onna, Cuba 1988.
9...♘xe4

9...♕xb2 10 ♖b1 ♕a3 11 ♘cb5 gives White play for the pawn; for example, 10...♕a5? (11...♕c5 was better) 12 ♘xc6 ♕xd2+ 13 ♔xd2 bxc6 14 ♘c7 and White should win, though amazingly Black managed to scramble a draw in J.Torremarin Gonzalez-M.Suba, St Cugat 1994.
10 fxe4 ♗xd4 11 ♗xd4 ♕xd4 12 ♕xd4 ♘xd4 13 0-0-0 ♘c6

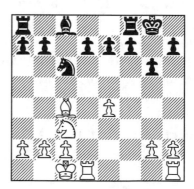

White's only compensation here is the temporary activity that comes from having fewer pawns to impede one's pieces.
14 h4 d6 15 ♘d5 ♗g4 16 ♖df1 ♗e6 17 h5 ♗xd5 18 ♗xd5 g5 19 ♖h3 h6?! 20 a4

Missing a chance to save herself with 20 ♖b3 ♖ab8 (and not 20...♘a5 because of 21 ♖b5) 21 ♖a3 ♖a8 22 ♖b3 e6 (it's either this or a draw by repetition) 23 ♗xc6 bxc6 24 ♖b7 and Black is tied down to both a7 and f7. Black should have prevented this possibility rather than consolidate his kingside with 19...h6.

20...Rab8 21 Rc3 Rbc8 22 Kb1 Kg7 23 Rb3 b6 24 Rc3 Ne5

Black is a pawn up and has the superior minor piece.

25 Ra3 e6 26 Ba2 Rc6 27 Rf2 Rfc8 28 a5 b5 29 a6 R8c7 30 Rd2 Kf6 31 Rf2+ Ke7 32 Ra5 Rb6 33 Bb3 Nc6 34 Ra3

Ne5 35 Ba2 b4 36 Rb3 Rc4 37 Re3 Rd4 38 Re1 Rxa6 39 Bb3 f6 40 Ref1 Ng4 41 Re2 Ra5 42 Rfe1 Rc5 43 Ba4 Ra5 44 Bb3 Re5 45 c3 bxc3 46 bxc3 Rd3 47 Kc2 Rg3 48 Kd2 Rb5 49 Bc2 Rc5 50 Ra1 a5 51 Bd3 Ne5 52 Ba6 Rgxc3 0-1

Key Points

1. Chess players are their own worst enemy and this enemy participates in every game. Self knowledge is therefore vitally important, but unfortunately it also requires self honesty. This can be the tricky part for many people.

2. Make a point of trying to understand how your opponents think and see if you can detect erroneous patterns. The Pavlovian reaction to fianchettos is just one example.

3. If you detect these patterns it can be worth tailoring your opening repertoire so as to exploit them.

Chapter Ten

Improve your Fitness Level

With chess games these days lasting anything up to seven hours it is more important than ever to be physically fit. But what kind of fitness is required?

Certainly there is no need to develop big muscles for chess, unless the powers that be suddenly introduce a requirement for very heavy pieces! It is far more important to be able to sit and concentrate for long periods of time, which is not the general goal of exercise. For this a good supply of oxygen should reach the brain and the muscles should be both reasonably toned and able to relax.

Are there any exercises that are particularly suitable for this? Indeed there are, but not traditional western forms. Instead, one must look to various eastern traditions such as yoga, qigong, and martial arts.

Yoga is an obvious choice because yogis cultivate the ability to sit and fo-

cus for hour after hour. Amongst today's top players I know that both Viswanathan Anand and Veselin Topalov practice yoga. Victor Korchnoi also had yoga instruction from the notorious Ananda Marga sect during his match with Anatoly Karpov in 1978, though I don't know the full extent of his interest.

There seems to be a particularly strong link between chess and martial arts, perhaps because both have a warrior link. I know that many of my students have an interest in martial arts, while amongst Grandmasters there is Yasser Seirawan (tai chi), Gata Kamsky (karate), Marcin Kaminski (kyokushin, tai chi and kung fu) and Maurice Ashley (aikido). The best known chess player/martial artist is Josh Waitzkin, who gained the International Master title before switching to tai chi and winning a world title.

How exactly does martial arts help? I suspect that the key elements are the focus on breathing, relaxation and posture, which most martial arts have to a greater or lesser extent. This is also something they have in common with yoga. These practices help to focus the mind and nervous system. Meanwhile the movements will gently tone the body.

It would be interesting to see if a study might confirm my anecdotal view on this. Certainly it seems that the yoga and martial arts practitioners have great stamina, as is in evidence in the following games by Kamsky and Seirawan.

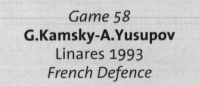

Game 58
G.Kamsky-A.Yusupov
Linares 1993
French Defence

1 e4 e6 2 d4 d5 3 ♘c3 ♗b4 4 e5 ♘e7 5 a3 ♗xc3+ 6 bxc3 c5 7 ♕g4 0-0 8 ♗d3 ♘bc6 9 ♕h5 ♘g6 10 ♘f3 ♕c7

11 ♗e3!?

A new move at the time, simply supporting his centre. White's alternatives are 11 0-0, 11 h4 and 11 ♘g5.

11...c4 12 ♗xg6 fxg6 13 ♕g4 ♕f7! 14 h4

Now Black gets to exchange queens, after which the odds of him getting mated diminish considerably. White could keep the queens on by playing 14 ♔d2!? so as to meet 14...♕f5 with 15 ♕g3.

14...♕f5 15 ♕xf5 ♖xf5 16 ♔e2 h6 17 g4 ♖f7 18 ♖ag1 ♗d7 19 ♘e1

Kamsky mentioned another possibility in his notes, which is to sacrifice a piece by 19 h5!? g5 20 ♘xg5 hxg5 21 ♗xg5, when it is difficult for Black to stop the white pawns advancing. I can only say that this is an easier line to suggest than to play.

19...♖af8 20 f4 ♖xf4?!

Yusupov was evidently getting anxious about White's pawn advance, but he does not have enough for the exchange. It would have been better to hang tough with 20...♗e8, after which

21 ♘g2 (21 h5? gxh5 22 ♖xh5 ♖xf4 is good for Black) 21...♖c7, intending 22...♘e7, gives both sides chances.

21 ♗xf4 ♖xf4 22 ♖g3! ♘d8 23 ♘g2 ♖f8 24 ♔e3 ♗a4 25 ♖c1?!

25 ♘e1 and 26 ♖f3 was a better way to unravel.

25...g5 26 hxg5 hxg5 27 ♖h3 ♘f7 28 ♖h5 ♖c8 29 ♘e1 ♖c6 30 ♖b1 ♖c7 31 ♔d2 ♗e8 32 ♘f3

White is finally getting round to attacking the weak pawn on g5.

32...♖e7

Had Black tried to trap White's rook with 32...♘h6? 33 ♖xg5 g6, then 34 ♘h4 followed by ♖f1-f6 would win the g6-pawn.

33 ♖bh1 ♖c7! 34 ♖h7 ♖c6 35 ♖1h5

Threatening 36 ♘xg5 ♘xg5 37 ♖h8+ followed by 38 ♖xg5. Black's reply is forced.

35...♖c8 36 ♔e3 a5 37 ♖h1

It would now be a mistake to play 37 ♘xg5?, as after 37...♘xg5 38 ♖h8+ ♔f7 39 ♖xg5 g6! 40 ♖h7+ ♔g8 41 ♖xb7 ♗f7 White's rook on g5 is trapped.

37...a4 38 ♖7h2 b5 39 ♖f2 ♖c7 40 ♖h5

♖e7 41 ♖f1 ♖b7 42 ♔f2! ♖b6?!

Allowing a breakthrough because Black's rook gets stuck defending the e6-pawn from the third rank. Black should have played 42...♖c7.

43 ♔g3 ♖a6 44 ♖xg5! ♘xg5 45 ♘xg5 ♗g6 46 ♖f2 ♖b6 47 ♔h4!

Preparing to force his way in on the kingside.

47...♖a6 48 ♘h3

48...♗e4

After something like 48...♖c6 49 ♘f4 ♗e4 50 ♔h5 ♖a6 51 ♘h3! ♖a7 52 ♘g5, White gets his desired position.

And 48...♔h7 allows him in at once with 49 ♖f8 ♗xc2 50 ♘g5+ ♔g6 51 ♖e8, when the attempted breakthrough by 51...b4!? 52 cxb4 ♗b3 fails to 53 ♖c8! ♖b6 54 ♖c7 ♖a6 55 b5! ♖b6 56 ♖c6 ♖xb5 57 ♖xe6 mate.

49 ♔h5! ♖a7 50 ♘g5 ♖e7 51 ♘xe4 dxe4 52 ♔g6 e3 53 ♖e2 ♖f7 54 ♖xe3 ♖f2 55 ♖e1!

The winning move, bringing the rook round to b1.

55...♖xc2 56 ♖b1 ♖xc3 57 ♖xb5 ♔f8 58 ♖b4 ♖xa3 59 ♖xc4 ♖a1 60 g5 a3 61 ♖a4

a2 62 ☖a7 ☗e8 63 ☗xg7 ☗d8 64 g6 ☗e8 65 ☖a6 ☗e7 66 ☖a8!

66...☗d7 67 ☗g8 ☗e7 68 ☖a7+ ☗e8 69 g7 ☖h1 70 ☖xa2 ☗e7 71 ☖a7+ ☗e8 72 ☖a5 ☗e7 73 d5 exd5 74 ☖xd5 ☖h2 75 ☖a5 ☖h1 76 ☖a7+ ☗e8 77 e6 ☖h2 78 ☖f7 ☖h1 79 e7 ☖h2 80 ☖f8+ ☗xe7 81 ☖f3 ☗e8 82 ☖e3+ ☗d7 83 ☖e4 1-0

Setting up the Lucena position as in Game 32. The winning procedure is 83...☖h1 84 ☗f7 ☖f1+ 85 ☗g6 ☖g1+ 86 ☗f6 ☖f1+ 87 ☗g5 ☖g1+ 88 ☖g4 etc.

Game 59
L.Portisch-Y.Seirawan
Dubai Olympiad 1986
Queen's Gambit Accepted

1 d4 d5 2 c4 dxc4 3 ☗f3 c5 4 e3 ☗f6 5 ☗xc4 e6 6 0-0 a6 7 ☗e2 b5 8 ☗d3 cxd4 9 exd4 ☗c6 10 a4 bxa4 11 ☖xa4 ☗b4 12 ☗c4 ☗e7 13 ☗g5 a5

A good move in a tricky position. 13...0-0 is met by 14 ☗xf6, when Black must take back with the pawn, so as to keep defending his knight on b4.

And after 13...☗fd5 White has 14 ☗xe7 ☗xe7 15 ☗b5+ ☗d7 16 ☗e5! ☗xb5 17 ☗xb5+, when Black must lose his castling rights.

14 ☗b5+ ☗d7 15 ☗e5 0-0

16 ☖xb4!?

The start of an interesting combination by Portisch. 16 ☗c3 would be pretty much equal after 16...☗xb5 17 ☗xb5 ☗fd5.

16...axb4 17 ☗xd7 ☗xd7 18 ☗c6 ☗xg5!

Black is forced to sacrifice his queen, not that this is bad for him. The resulting position is rock solid.

19 ☗xd8 ☖fxd8 20 ☗b5 ☗e7 21 ☗d2 ☗f6

22 ♘f3

22 ♘b3!? might have been better.

22...♖db8 23 ♕e2 ♖c8 24 ♘e5 ♘d5 25 ♖e1

Threatening 26 ♘xf7, but of course Seirawan spots that.

25...♖f8! 26 ♘c6 ♖fc8 27 ♘e5 ♖f8 28 g3 ♗f6 29 ♘c6 ♖a2 30 ♖b1 ♖fa8

And not 30...♘c3? because of 31 ♕c4!.

31 ♕b5 g6 32 ♔g2 ♔g7 33 ♕b7 ♖a1! 34 ♖xa1 ♖xa1

35 ♕b5?!

At this stage Portisch was probably playing for a win, but he should have settled for 35 ♘xb4 ♘xb4 36 ♕xb4, when 36...♖d1 followed by ...♗xd4, ...e6-e5 and ...♖b1 will be a draw.

35...♖b1 36 ♕e2 ♖c1 37 ♘a5 h5 38 ♘b3 ♖c7 39 ♕e4 ♘e7 40 ♘d2 ♖d7 41 ♘f3 ♖d5 42 ♕c2 ♘f5 43 ♕c4 ♘xd4 44 ♕xb4 ♘xf3 45 ♔xf3 ♖d4 46 ♕b5 ♖d2 47 b4?!

Letting the wrong pawn go. Instead, 47 ♔e3 ♖xb2 48 ♕c4 should be a draw.

47...♗d4 48 ♕d7 ♖xf2+ 49 ♔e4 e5 50 h3 ♖e2+ 51 ♔f3 ♖f2+ 52 ♔e4 ♖e2+ 53 ♔f3 ♖e1 54 ♔g2 ♖g1+ 55 ♔f3 ♖f1+ 56 ♔e4 ♖e1+ 57 ♔f3 ♖e3+ 58 ♔g2 ♖d3 59 ♕c6 ♖d2+ 60 ♔f1 ♗f2+ 61 ♔e1 ♖f6³ 62 ♕d5 ♗f2+ 63 ♔e2 ♗xg3 64 b5 ♖f2+ 65 ♔d1 ♖f1+ 66 ♔c2 ♖f6 67 ♔d2 h4 68 ♕c5 ♖f2+ 69 ♔d1 ♖f1+ 70 ♔d2 ♖f2+ 71 ♔d1 ♖f1+ 72 ♔d2 ♗f4+ 73 ♔e2 ♖b1 74 b6 ♖b2+ 75 ♔d1?!

After this White's king is trapped on the back rank. 75 ♔d3 instead was a better try.

75...g5 76 ♕c7 g4 77 ♕c8 g3

78 ♕g4+??

A blunder in time trouble. White could have fought on with 78 b7, when 78...g2 79 ♕g4+ ♔f6 80 ♕xg2 ♖xg2 81 b8♕ ♔g7 leaves Black with all the chances, but also a lot of work.

78...♔f6 79 ♕xh4+ ♔g6 80 ♕g4+ ♔f6 81 ♕h4+ ♔e6 82 ♕g4+ ♔d6 83 b7 ♖xb7 84 ♔c2 ♖b6! 85 h4 ♔e7 86 h5 ♖d6! 87 ♔c3 ♖d2 88 ♕h4+

88 h6 is met by 88...♖h2, winning the pawn.

88...♔e8 89 ♕g4 g2 90 ♕g8+ ♔e7 91 ♕g7 e4 92 ♔c4 ♗h2 93 ♕g5+ ♔e6 94 ♕h6+ ♔f5 95 ♕h7+ ♔g5 96 ♕g7+ ♔h4 97 ♕f6+ ♔g4 98 ♕g7+ ♔h3 0-1

Case History: Nigel Davies

My interest in qigong and martial arts started two and a half years ago when I was very much at a low ebb. I had put on a lot of weight, had very little energy for anything, and felt a pervading sense of vulnerability. All of this manifested itself in my chess, I was playing just horribly. Something had to be done!

The sense of vulnerability was something that particularly bothered me. Chess players, especially the good ones, tend to be an independent and self-reliant bunch, travelling the globe to fight it out for their dinner. So I started investigating different forms of martial arts.

My early research gave me cause for concern that, as a very overweight 40-something, I was likely to get injured. But eventually I discovered a safer-looking form of training which entailed standing still. Now what could be hard about that?

It turned out that I had stumbled across one of the most demanding forms of exercise known to man. Zhan zhuang ("post standing") involves standing still in various postures for huge tracts of time, which is much harder than it may sound. At one time kept secret, it was introduced to Europe by Master Lam Kam Chuen in 1987.

As the weeks and months of practice went by I experienced all kinds of discomfort, from dull pain to sweating,

shaking and flatulence. But still I stood.

An old ankle injury made its presence felt, but then started to improve again until I found I could run for the first time in a decade. I also found myself becoming much calmer, my need for comfort eating and drinking gradually disappeared, and over time I lost 25 kilos (about 4 stone).

The effect on my chess was equally dramatic as the following games testify. The first three show how dreadfully I was playing at the New England Chess Masters in August 2007. But the last two games show a return to some decent form, with wins over GM Aaron Summerscale in the Four Nations Chess League and then Willy Hendriks at the 2009 Staunton Memorial.

Game 60
N.Davies-J.Critelli
New England Masters,
Peabody 2007
Réti Opening

1 ♘f3 ♘f6 2 g3 d5 3 ♗g2 e6 4 0-0 ♗e7 5 d3 b6 6 ♘bd2 ♗b7 7 e4 dxe4?!

A fairly common error in this type of position: when White plays e4-e5 he will get the e4-square for his knights.
8 dxe4 0-0 9 ♕e2 c5 10 e5 ♘fd7 11 ♘e4 ♕c7 12 ♗f4 ♖d8 13 ♘f6+!

I've played this sacrifice before in similar positions, but on this occasion I was having trouble calculating it out. This is more evident on my 15th move.

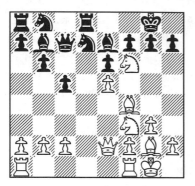

13...gxf6?

This should lose, providing White plays well. Black's best defence was 13...♘xf6 14 exf6 ♗d6, though this leads to a serious weakening of his king position after 15 ♗xd6 ♖xd6 16 fxg7.

14 exf6 ♗d6 15 ♘d4?

Missing an immediate win via 15 ♗xd6! ♕xd6 16 ♘g5, when 16...♗xg2 17 ♕h5 leads to mate after 17...♘xf6 18 ♕xf7+ ♔h8 19 ♕xf6+ ♔g8 20 ♕f7+ ♔h8 21 ♕xh7 mate.

15...cxd4 16 ♗xb7?

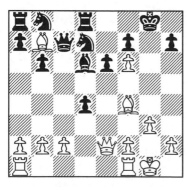

And this hands the game over on a silver platter. The best chance was 16 ♕g4+, after which 16...♔f8 17 ♗xd6+

♕xd6 18 ♕g7+ ♔e8 19 ♗xb7 ♘c6 20 ♗xa8 ♖xa8 21 ♕xh7 would have left me with fighting chances.

16...♗xf4 17 ♗xa8 ♗e5 18 ♕g4+ ♔f8 19 ♕g7+ ♔e8 20 ♕h8+?!

Another bad move. 20 ♗g2 ♗xf6 21 ♕xh7 was relatively better.

20...♘f8 21 ♗e4 ♘bd7 22 ♗xh7??

A final blunder. 22 ♕g7 would at least allow the queen to escape.

22...♗xf6 23 ♕g8 ♔e7! 24 ♗d3 ♘e5 0-1

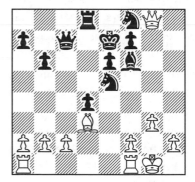

The white queen cannot retreat and will be trapped by ...♘fg6 and ...♖h8.

Game 61
M.Enkin-N.Davies
New England Masters,
Peabody 2007
Sicilian Defence

1 e4 c5 2 ♘f3 g6 3 d4 cxd4 4 ♕xd4 ♘f6 5 e5 ♘c6 6 ♕a4 ♘d5 7 ♕e4 ♘c7

To be honest I had forgotten what Black was supposed to do in this line and was making it up as I went along. The usual move is 7...♘db4, though this

leads to enormous complications after 8 ♗b5 ♕a5 9 ♘c3 d5 10 exd6 ♗f5 11 ♗xc6+ bxc6 (11...♘xc6 may be better; for example 12 ♕d5 exd6 13 0-0 ♕xd5!? 14 ♘xd5 ♗d7 15 c3 ♗g7 and Black's useful bishop pair compensates for his inferior pawn structure) 12 d7+ ♔d8 13 ♕c4 ♘xc2+ 14 ♔e2 with a wild position.
8 ♘c3 ♗g7 9 ♗c4 b5!? 10 ♗xb5 ♘xb5 11 ♘xb5 ♕a5+ 12 ♘c3

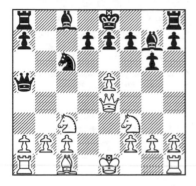

12...♗xe5

With more energy I might have delayed regaining my pawn in favour of the dynamic 12...♖b8, unpinning the knight on c6. The position looks quite promising for Black after 13 0-0 ♗b7 14 ♕e3 ♘b4 because of the enormous activity of his pieces.
13 ♘xe5 ♕xe5 14 ♕xe5 ♘xe5 15 ♘d5 ♖b8

Here, too, I missed a more promising line in 15...♗b7!?, after which 16 ♘c7+ ♔d8 17 ♘xa8 ♗xg2 18 ♖f1 ♘f3+ 19 ♔e2 ♘d4+ 20 ♔d3 ♗xf1+ 21 ♔xd4 ♗g2 emerges with an extra pawn.
16 ♗f4 f6 17 0-0-0 ♗b7 18 ♘e3 d6 19 ♗xe5 fxe5 20 ♖he1 0-0 21 ♖d2 ♔g7

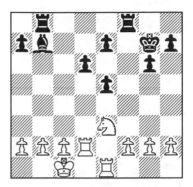

Black is slightly better here due to his strong bishop, but it won't be easy to win.
22 c4 ♖f4 23 b3 g5 24 h3 ♔g6 25 ♔b2 ♖bf8 26 ♖ee2 h5 27 ♔c3 g4 28 hxg4 hxg4 29 b4 ♖c8 30 ♔b3 ♔g5 31 a4 ♖d4 32 ♔c3 ♗xg2!? 33 ♖xd4 exd4+ 34 ♔xd4 ♗f3 35 ♖d2 ♔f4 36 ♘d5+ ♗xd5 37 cxd5 ♔f3 38 a5 ♖c1 39 a6 ♖f1?!

Frustration mixes in with tiredness and I start to go over the top. The right move was 39...♖b1, when 40 ♔c4 ♖c1+ 41 ♔b5 ♖f1 42 ♔c6 ♖xf2 43 ♖xf2+ ♔xf2 44 b5 g3 45 b6 axb6 46 a7 g2 47 a8♕ g1♕ 48 ♕f8+ is drawing.
40 b5

40...♖xf2??

And this is another horrible blunder. 40...♖b1 is the only chance, though by now Black is fighting for his life.

41 ♖xf2+ ♔xf2 42 b6 g3 43 bxa7 g2 44 a8♕ g1♕ 45 ♕c6

White's second a-pawn decides the game.

45...♔f3+ 46 ♔c4 ♔e4 47 ♔b5 ♔e5 48 ♕b6 ♕f1+ 49 ♔c6 ♕c4+ 50 ♔d7 ♕a4+ 51 ♔c7 ♔xd5 52 ♕b7+ 1-0

Game 62
L.Milman-N.Davies
New England Masters,
Peabody 2007
Sicilian Defence

1 e4 c5 2 ♘f3 g6 3 d4 cxd4 4 ♘xd4 ♘c6 5 ♘c3 ♗g7 6 ♗e3 ♘f6 7 ♗c4 ♕a5 8 0-0 0-0 9 a3 d6 10 h3 ♗d7 11 f4 ♕c5 12 ♕d3 ♘g4! 13 hxg4 ♗xd4 14 ♗xd4 ♕xd4+ 15 ♕xd4 ♘xd4 16 ♘d5

After this Black is better already. White should play 16 ♖ad1, when 16...e5 is approximately equal.

16...♗xg4 17 c3

Black is also doing well after 17 ♘xe7+ ♔g7; for example, 18 ♗d3 ♖ae8 19 ♘d5 f5 breaks up White's pawn duo on e4 and f4.

17...♘c6 18 f5 ♔h8 19 ♗b5 e6 20 ♘e3 ♘e5 21 ♘xg4 ♘xg4 22 fxe6 fxe6 23 ♗d7 ♘f6 24 ♗xe6 ♘xe4 25 ♖fe1 ♘f6 26 ♖ad1 ♖fe8 27 ♗b3

27 ♖xd6 ♖e7, followed by 28...♖ae8, would leave White in an unpleasant pin on the e-file.

27...♖xe1+ 28 ♖xe1 ♖e8 29 ♖d1?!

White should probably exchange rooks rather than allow Black to get to the seventh rank.

29...♖e2 30 ♖xd6 ♖xb2 31 ♖xf6 ♖xb3 32 ♖f7 ♖xc3 33 ♖xb7 ♖xa3

Two pawns up in the endgame should be a simple matter of technique for a Grandmaster such as myself, shouldn't it? But this does not prove to be the case.

34 ♔h2 h5 35 ♖c7 ♔g8 36 ♖b7 ♔f8 37 ♖c7 a5 38 ♖a7 a4 39 ♔g1 ♖a2

It would be much easier to win if I'd have kept the rook on the sixth rank.

After 39...h4 40 ♔h2 ♔e8 41 ♔g1 (or 41 ♖h7 g5 42 ♖g7 ♖g3 43 ♖a7 a3 44 ♔h1 ♔d8) 41...g5, Black is ready to march his king to b8.

40 ♔h2 ♖a3 41 ♔g1 ♖a1+

41...h4 is still possible, with what looks like an easy win.

42 ♔h2 a3

42...♖a3 would have been a good move had it not created a threefold repetition. So 42...♔g8 may be the best way.

43 ♔g3

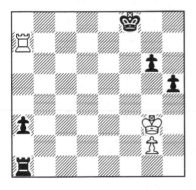

43...a2?

A lazy move that makes Black's rook really bad. I should have played 43...g5, when 44 ♖a6 ♔e7 45 ♖a7+ ♔d6 46 ♖a6+ ♔c5 leaves the a2-square for the king.

44 ♔h2 h4 45 ♖a3 ♔g7 46 ♖a7+ ♔h6 47 ♖a5 g5 48 ♖a6+ ♔h5 49 ♖a4 ♔g6 50 ♖a8 ♔f6 51 ♖a5 ♔e6 52 ♖a8 ♔d5 53 ♖a4 g4 54 g3 ♖d1

Fritz loves 54...hxg3+ but does not explain how Black should get his king safe from checks.

55 ♖xa2 h3 56 ♖a5+ ♔e4 57 ♖e5+ ½-½

Game 63
N.Davies-W.Hendriks
Staunton Memorial,
London 2009
Sicilian Defence

1 g3

The sign of a player who does not like the well-trodden paths.

1...c5 2 ♗g2 g6 3 e4 ♗g7 4 f4 ♘c6 5 ♘f3

5...d6

Later in the tournament Eelke Wiersma played 5...e6 against me, the game continuing 6 0-0 ♘ge7 7 c3 0-0 8 ♘a3 b6 9 d4 cxd4 10 cxd4 f5 11 e5 ♗a6 12 ♖e1 b5 13 ♘c2 ♖c8 14 ♘d2 ♘a5 15 b3 ♗b7 16 ♗a3 ♗xg2 17 ♔xg2 ♖e8 18 ♘e3 ♘b7 19 ♘f3 d5 20 ♕d2 ½-½.

6 0-0 ♘f6 7 d3 0-0 8 ♘c3 ♖b8 9 h3 b5 10 g4 b4 11 ♘e2 a5

An earlier game of mine had proceeded 11...♘e8 12 f5 ♘c7 13 ♕e1 ♘b5 14 ♕h4 ♘bd4 15 ♘exd4 ♘xd4 16 ♘xd4 ♗xd4+ 17 ♔h1 ♗b7 18 ♖b1 a5 19 ♗h6 ♕c7!? 20 ♗xf8 ♖xf8, when Black had compensation for the exchange in N.Davies-I.Ivanov, London Lloyds Bank 1992.

12 ℤb1 c4 13 ♗e3 ♗a6 14 ℤf2

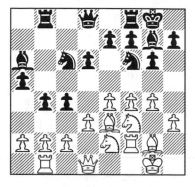

Evacuating the a6-f1 diagonal in order to inhibit Black's play. My opponent responds with a pawn sacrifice.

14...b3 15 axb3 cxd3 16 cxd3 ♘b4 17 ♘e1 ℤc8 18 f5

With the queenside stable I decided to proceed on the opposite flank.

18...♕c7 19 ♕d2 ♕b8 20 ℤa1 ♘c6 21 ♗h6 ♕xb3 22 ♗xg7 ♔xg7 23 ♘g3 ♕b6 24 ♔h2 ♘b4 25 d4 ℤc4 26 ℤd1 ♗b7 27 g5 ♘d7 28 f6+

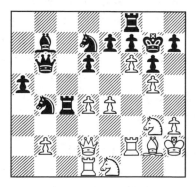

28...exf6?

Letting me in. Black should play 28...♔g8, when 29 fxe7 ℤe8 30 ♘f1 ℤxe7 is still balanced.

29 gxf6+ ♔h8

After 29...♘xf6 30 ♘f5+ ♔h8 (30...gxf5 31 ♕g5+ ♔h8 32 ♕xf6+ ♔g8 33 ℤxf5 is devastating) 31 ♕h6 ℤg8 32 ♘e3 White wins material.

30 ♕h6 ℤg8 31 ♘f3 ♘f8 32 ♘g5 ♕c7 33 ℤf4 ℤc2 34 ℤg1 1-0

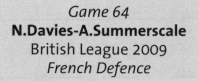

Game 64
N.Davies-A.Summerscale
British League 2009
French Defence

1 e4 e6 2 d3 d5 3 ♘d2 c5 4 g3 ♘c6 5 ♗g2 g6 6 ♘h3

This is very much my territory. In such positions the knight is effectively placed here because it can cooperate with its colleague to support e5. The knight on d2 can come to f3, while the one on h3 can go to f2 and g4.

6...♗g7 7 0-0 ♘ge7 8 f4 0-0 9 e5 f6 10 exf6 ♗xf6 11 ♘f3 ♕d6 12 ♘f2

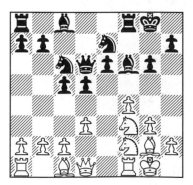

It may be worth rereading my previous note. White now wishes to play ♘f2-g4, which Black prevents by advancing in the centre. But this in turn brings additional responsibilities.

12...e5 13 c3 ♗d7 14 ♔h1 ♗g7

Fritz 12 experiences some confusion here. After liking 14...♖ae8 for a while, it promptly changes its mind given 15 fxe5 ♘xe5 16 ♗f4. I can only assume my computer is not powerful enough for poor *Fritz* to understand my 'White is better' assessment.

15 fxe5 ♘xe5 16 ♗f4 g5

Perhaps Black's best chance was 16...♖xf4, just sacrificing the exchange to confuse the issue.

17 ♗xe5

Keeping an edge without allowing counterplay. Objectively speaking 17 ♘xg5 looks stronger, though I was concerned about the possibility of 17...h6 18 ♘f3 ♖xf4 19 gxf4 ♘5g6 with play for the exchange.

17...♗xe5 18 ♘xe5 ♕xe5

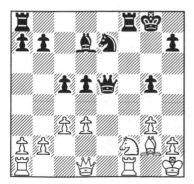

19 ♕h5 ♕g7 20 ♖ae1 ♖f6

Maybe 20...♖ad8 was a better try.

21 ♘g4 ♖d6 22 ♘e5 ♗e6 23 ♗h3 ♗xh3 24 ♕xh3 ♘c6

Or 24...♖f8 25 ♘d7 ♖xf1+ 26 ♖xf1, threatening 27 ♖f8+ and 27 ♘xc5.

25 ♖f7 ♕h6 26 ♕f1 ♖e8

Losing, but Black is under strong pressure in any case. After 26...♘xe5 27 ♖xe5 ♖e6 White plays 28 ♖ff5; for example, 28...♖xe5 29 ♖xe5 ♖f8 30 ♕e2 ♕g6 31 ♕e3 h6 32 ♕xc5 ♕xd3 33 ♕xd5+ with an extra pawn in the rook endgame.

27 ♘g4 ♖xe1 28 ♘xh6+ ♖xh6 29 ♖f8+ ♔g7 30 ♕xe1 ♔xf8 31 ♕f2+ ♔e7 32 ♕xc5+ ♖d6 33 ♔g2 h6 34 b4 ♔d7 35 b5 ♘e5 36 ♕xa7 ♔c7 37 ♕e3 ♘d7 38 a4 b6 39 ♕e7 ♖f6 40 c4 ♖d6 1-0

Despite its deadly dull appearance (there's even less activity than in chess games) taking up zhan zhuang has been one of the most exciting things I have done in the last decade. Recently I also started practising the complimentary art of tai chi, which is incredibly fast moving by comparison. I currently train for two to three hours per day.

Westerners have difficulty appreciating exercise without muscle or testosterone, so these systems will not easily be understood. But they way they harmonize mind, body and breath can produce profound benefits.

Key Points

1. The way that someone's chess is going is often a litmus test for their physical and emotional well being.

2. Unless someone already has great physical and emotional stamina they can improve their chess a great deal via yoga, qigong or martial arts.

3. Taking up one of these art forms can also improve your health and life as a whole.

4. Most people dabble, but then the effect will be limited. To gain the most benefit you should choose one method and then practice it seriously. Remember that a master is just a beginner who never gave up.

Index of Openings

Figures refer to page numbers.

Index of Games and Positions